WHY CAN'T YOU HEAR ME?

WHY CAN'T YOU HEAR ME?

My Recovery from Borderline Personality Disorder & Anorexia Nervosa

By Gisel Josy

Cherish
EDITIONS

First published in Great Britain 2021 by Cherish Editions

Cherish Editions is a trading style of Shaw Callaghan Ltd & Shaw Callaghan

23 USA, INC.The Foundation Centre, Navigation House, 48 Millgate, Newark

Nottinghamshire NG24 4TS UK

www.triggerhub.org

Text Copyright © Gisel Josy

British Library Cataloguing in Publication Data

A CIP catalogue record for this book is available upon request from the British Library

ISBN: 9781913615116

This book is also available in eBook format: 9781913615123

Gisel Josy has asserted her right under the Copyright, Design and Patents Act 1988 to be
identified as the author of this work

Cover design by Bookollective

Typeset by Lapiz Digital Services

Cherish Editions encourages diversity and different viewpoints. However, all views, thoughts and opinions expressed in this book are the author's own and are not necessarily representative of us as an organisation.

All material in this book is set out in good faith for general guidance and no liability can be accepted for loss or expense incurred in following the information given. In particular this book is not intended to replace expert medical or psychiatric advice. It is intended for informational purposes only and for your own personal use and guidance. It is not intended to act as a substitute for professional medical advice. The author is not a medical practitioner nor a counsellor, and professional advice should be sought if desired before embarking on any health-related programme.

Contents

INTRODUCTION
Title explained

You can hear the outrage, eruption of anger and frustration that has built up overtime, because anorexia not only starves the body, but the mind and soul too, so staying not only sane but also yourself becomes the real battle.

You can hear the cry for help when anorexia suppresses any speck of hope and replaces it with delusional beliefs that will never live up to expectations.

You can hear your child abiding to every command this illness orders them to do, despite the fact it is compromising their health, wellbeing and happiness. As they are blinded by the false promises anorexia uses to entice each vulnerable victim.

You can hear your child reciting the calories of the groceries that you just bought as though it was a prayer. The meals they once enjoyed and would eagerly sit down to eat around the dining table with family are now replaced by disgust, uneasiness and an evergrowing mountain of lies such as, "I've already had my lunch." Anorexia grabs hold of the steering wheel and doesn't fail to bite back, even in the most unexpected and unwanted times.

You can hear your child panting heavily after exercising for hours on end as a punishment for eating too much and even the sound of them throwing up after every meal seeps through the bathroom walls.

You can hear the distress and sheer panic in their voice when they are put on the spot and made to conjure up a believable lie when questioned about the packet of laxatives stashed in their schoolbag.

But why can't you hear me?
Gisel Josy.

The person behind this story. Don't be fooled into thinking that I am nothing more than the behaviours I exhibit and the struggles that I went through. I am a human, with a name, interests, a personality and, more importantly, the ability to change the world for the better, just like anyone else can.

Why did I choose to start writing?

The idea of writing a diary, let alone a book, never occurred to me. Now I realise that a thought process had been triggered a couple of weeks before I started jotting down ideas. I spent most of my afternoons in a library brimming with books. There was a wide range, including fiction, literature and even on how to learn a language. However, I was quite astonished, and somewhat disheartened, by the fact that only about half a shelf within this two-storey library was dedicated to mental health – a battle we all combat during our lifetime, one way or another. I sensed a scope within the market for books that talked openly about mental health which would deepen our understanding around it and how it is easily misinterpreted as something to be ashamed of, when that shouldn't be the case. I hope this book in some ways acts as an incentive and motivation to spur you on through recovery and to let those suffering know that they are not alone in this battle. And that they shouldn't be made to feel any different or scrutinized for having a mental disorder, especially one that has often been categorised as self-inflicted within society i.e. anorexia.

The journey begins

Life is unpredictable; the uncertainties make up our highs and lows for the day. Differences make you unique within a crowd and similarities unite a community. But above all, love, respect and showcasing acceptance or acknowledgement of one's views and beliefs, even if it doesn't seem viable or is contradictory to yours, is key. This is the mindset we all need to adopt in order to eradicate the stigma surrounding mental health. Being able to understand is the first step to this, but accepting that we are all victims of deteriorating mental health at some point in our lives is crucial. This does not necessarily mean that there is a label (official diagnosis) that is plastered all over your health records, rather acknowledging that we've all had our bad days.

As a child growing up in the bustling multicultural city of London, I was faced with technological advances on a regular basis. This catered to people's ever-growing needs in this evolving world. Today, many children use technology as a prime source of pleasure, as a way of learning and a means of interaction or communication. However, as much as I tried to fit into this world and meet its expectations, I was unable to keep it up for very long. Sitting behind a computer screen with my eyes wide-open, glaring as though I was in a trance, was not for me.

This realisation prompted me to try new things in the hope of finding my true passion, which was reading. To some, this was simply seen as 'nerdy' and not something someone of my age would engage in. Reading habits are on the decline and libraries have unfortunately become sparse. It is falsely depicted as a time-consuming, solitary and tiresome experience that can be replaced "effectively" by films. We fail to realise that books are, in fact, a fountain of knowledge and existed before the first television was invented. It provides us with a wealth of knowledge that helps us to comment on issues of today and show us what the future might hold. It would be foolish to disregard the importance and usefulness of books.

With this in mind nothing was able to deter me from spending my afternoons in the library engrossed in books – in particular, fictional stories – for countless hours. In hindsight,

I assume I opted for fictional books because the storyline was a sugar-coated version of reality and had the prospect of a happy ending, which every child wanted to hear. However, not only as I grew in age but maturity and life experience too, one thing I had lost over the years was my sense of optimism. It was replaced with growing mistrust, doubt and concern about anything and everything. I soon realised that fantasy stories were far from the truth; they were simply there to spark the imagination and curiosity of the young whilst having an underlying moral that could be applicable to the real world. It's everyone's dream to have a happily ever after but it is often a far-fetched reality that only happens in story books. That is not to say we can't create our own happily ever after. It may not comprise of a prince charming, a golden treasure chest and a fairy god mother to confide to, but instead creating memories with the people you love and achieving things that were out of your reach.

I want to clarify that this book will not cure you. There is, worryingly, no cure for this illness yet, unlike a tumour that can be surgically removed, a fractured leg that can be placed in a cast or an infection that can be treated with a course of antibiotics. Any medication from antidepressants to antipsychotics ingested, injected or even nasogastrically tubed does not resolve the problem, because the illness is inseparable. It is you, and your mind alone, which has become your worst enemy, though cunningly disguised as your best friend as well.

In this book, we will explore the meaning of Anorexia Nervosa from a sufferer's point of view, rather than it being a bog-standard dictionary definition, supported by statistical analysis and research studies by top scholars with limited or no first-hand experience. This is of very little use when trying to understand even a fraction of the sheer pain a loved one may be enduring and why all of a sudden, a numerical value has destroyed the foundations that once built your family or friendship, and made way to birthdays, holidays and even

Christmas becoming painstakingly hard to enjoy. Instead it has been replaced with mistrust, doubt and growing separation.

As you look into your little girl's eyes, there is no longer a hazel brown glimmer, rather eyes that have been drained of colour and life. Her protruding bones makes her unable to sit or sleep comfortably for more than ten minutes at a time. Family dinners have become a thing of the past, and her genuine smile and wittiness appears to be a fading memory.

There are always misconceptions around what anorexia recovery should entail and whether it is plausible for all. The concept is similar to a maths question, in that there are several processes or methods that can be undertaken to get to the final answer, with people taking different lengths of time to do so. But the process or time taken should not be scrutinized nor dismissed as being right or wrong, as there is no correct way of doing recovery. It is very much individualized, aligned to the future you wish to have and the incentives you have around you to stimulate this.

Recovery enables you to create stable relationships that can pull you through difficult times, rather than resorting to destructive behaviours that exacerbate the grasp anorexia has on you. This grasp overrules even your most domineering and long-held values and ethics. Treasured memories held close to your heart start to dissipate. Being yourself becomes exceptionally hard and an unfamiliar sight to others.

CHAPTER 1

What is Anorexia Nervosa?

The "ideal" body shape

Before we delve into the details of this highly misunderstood mental health condition known as Anorexia Nervosa, it is important to remember that this condition targets a wide range of people of any nationality, race, gender, age and sexuality. It is known to be a notorious killer for those aged between fifteen and twenty-five. Suicide rates are surging and those combatting an eating disorder are more likely to commit suicide. In fact, 1 in 4 of those affected commit suicide because of the fear of being a burden to others; they do not do it as a selfish act but as a selfless act. It is a desperate cry for help and can seem like the only way to cease a never-ending life of pain.

Over the years, we have witnessed vast progression in technology, breakthrough cures that have prevented epidemics and many scientific revelations. All of which has contributed to broadening our knowledge of the world around us. However, there has also been a drastic change that has affected a large proportion of the world's population, if not all, at some point in their lives. This is the notion of how women and men should ideally look, in the context of the culture or fashion of a particular era and location. Media exposure and celebrity endorsement have implemented this notion and helped to manipulate the insecurities of many around their bodies, in return for boosting the economy and finding fame. It is evident that many are lost in the pursuit of achieving what is perceived to be the "perfect" body, willing to jeopardise health and wellbeing for something that is actually unattainable.

How has society's perception of the ideal body changed for both women and men over time?

If we date back to the Renaissance, women who were full-figured and clinically overweight were seen as being the most attractive, because a thin figure had the negative connotations of being financially compromised and food-deprived. However, in the Victorian era, it was the fashion to wear corsets with tiny twelve-inch waists – a bizarre concept that left women with breathing difficulties and fractured ribs. Then came the model movement of the 1960s, in which women strived to be as skinny as possible, simply because skinny was the new trend. Later on, in the 1980s, women were tied up with achieving a toned physique known as the aerobic body, attained by adopting a diet culture and dedicating most of your life to the gym. Nowadays, the trends go back and forth between embracing curves and wanting to attain a skinny body. These unrealistic expectations have contributed to the rise of eating disorders and the surge in the unnecessary use of cosmetic surgery. The notion of the ideal body, for both men and women, needs to be eradicated, otherwise society will not be able to progress. Instead, the importance of being comfortable in your own skin should be emphasized. A change needs to happen in order for us to set the right example for future generations so that they do not have to contend with the same problems again and again. This change needs to happen right now, not in a year's time, not tomorrow, but now. The power is in our hands. We need to work in collaboration to instigate the change and see the benefits of it unfold.

In addition, we need to be aware of the fact that social pressure related to appearance is not only directed at women, but men as well, although it may not appear as obvious to the public eye. This matter can often be trivialised or completely disregarded.

Indeed, having a toned physique is often misconceived as a way of portraying masculinity. It can come as a shock when a young man in the 21st century does not engage in weight training to attain a muscular physique. For those that do choose to do so, it may even become an unhealthy obsession whereby they live, sleep and breathe the gym. The purpose becomes less about losing weight and more about putting your body through torture to strive for a physical ideal that isn't you. Every aspect of life revolves around your body, from scanning food items for the protein content or number of calories, to spending countless hours in the gym on your best friend's birthday, when you should be out enjoying their company. This endless pursuit to be "healthy" or "fitter" has stemmed from all sorts of insecurities, from childhood and current circumstances, as a way of coping with a substantial change. I have met a few young men that are living with the devastating consequences of bullying and trauma experienced in their early years, which led to the manifestation of an eating disorder and an enormous amount of grief. But replacing an eating disorder with a gym obsession – which can seem appealing due to the feeling that you are "regaining control" without gaining weight – is not the answer and will not aid your recovery. A gym obsession is just as disordered and is far from what recovery should entail. Abiding by rigid rules around how your body should look is a means of keeping the eating disorder alive and depriving your body of its basic needs. That said, we should not assume that men who go to the gym regularly have an eating disorder – it may just be a trait within their personality and hold a completely different purpose for them.

All in all, the "ideal" body and desired aesthetics play a crucial role for many, some as young as five years old, to teenagers undergoing puberty and, surprisingly, older generations, too. What is particularly worrying is that the term 'anorexic' is used as an adjective to describe one's appearance, both as a label to aspire to and as an insult. However, in my eyes, anorexia is so much more than what can be seen on the exterior. Many professionals are left oblivious to the adverse and prolonged effects of the disorder on patients and their loved one's lives. A definition that suits it better is "a befriending yet deceitful mental illness that tears down long-standing relationships, leaving fragmented families and lives." It can also have life-threatening health complications and make sufferers more prone to self-harm and compensatory behaviours. This is because a malnourished brain is found to heighten Emotional Dysregulation, as well as vulnerability and sensitivity to criticism or differences of opinion. Unfortunately, 20 per cent of those left untreated fall victim to anorexia's grasp and are at increased risk of death. There are also those who attempt to lead a life in the community while clinging onto anorexia, as they know nothing better. There are many reasons behind the success of anorexia's grasp; for example: severe malnutrition – depriving the body of its basic needs – facilitates the sense of satisfaction when a number on a scale plummets.

I was a girl with heaps of excitement and optimism for the future. I was able to immerse myself in books for hours on end without losing concentration, while being a social butterfly who dedicated time for family and friends, and made so many fond memories.

In contrast, anorexia "gifted" me with unbearable hunger cues and cravings; a burdening feeling of guilt and unworthiness, which would interrupt the rest of my day; social anxiety, especially in settings where food was unavoidable;

and ruminating over food all day, every day, which meant that everything else in life became invisible. Anorexia dictates that hunger cues should be ignored otherwise you will balloon over the course of a day. It cleverly replaces food with a cup of hot water to suppress these cravings without consuming any calories. "Bingo!" says anorexia, joyfully, each time. "In fact, you might as well do another 200 sit-ups for even having that unfathomable thought!". Anorexia not only consumes your thoughts, alters your thinking process and diminishes decisiveness, it damages spontaneity and socialising and any other attributes and hobbies that make up your identity. It cunningly manifests itself to look, sound and feel like you to the point where it is indistinguishable to yourself. It lurks in the background during recovery, ready to take advantage of a challenging or stressful point in your journey.

Anorexia is often just the tip of the iceberg and does not paint a full picture of the underlying struggles the individual may be facing. It is usually a coping mechanism, which, in turn, produces an emotional response to either unexpected or drastic changes in someone's life. It is most definitely not a lifestyle choice nor a diet gone wrong, and the intention from the start is not to become a bag of bones, but to be in "control" of at least one aspect of life. I contained myself within this safety blanket so I couldn't get hurt anymore. It gave me the answers to the questions that no one else was able to answer, such as, "Am I good enough?"

Similar to cancer, Anorexia Nervosa is an umbrella term and the issues are different from patient to patient. Treatment plans are tailored to each individual's care, depending on the stage of treatment. Physical and mental health risks indicate a rough timescale for recovery and which setting is best. A commitment to following an adequate meal plan, and concordance to medication and the long-term plan all play a part, too. You would not group bowel cancer with prostate or ovarian cancer, for example. They are treated as two different illnesses that target different parts of the body entirely – one is associated with the digestive system and the other is part of the reproductive system. Nonetheless, they all require attentive care and specialised treatment. The same applies for Anorexia Nervosa, whereby behaviours may range from over-exercising to abusing laxatives, though sufferers tend to share an overwhelming fear of weight gain due partly to low self-esteem. It is of great importance that sufferers seek help immediately, regardless of their BMI or whether they consider themselves to be "ill enough" for treatment. The sad fact is that some sufferers believe their problem isn't worth mentioning and this can be fatal.

As a result, many find themselves trapped in a vicious cycle of restriction or purging, or other deadly behaviours, which tightens the hold anorexia has on them. This delays their real recovery, hence why it takes, on average, six years for someone to fully recover.

It is also not uncommon to find individuals who are intellectually bright and strong easily tricked into obeying the orders dictated by this illness, which only wants each victim to become a lifeless person six-feet underground, covered in rubble and dirt, soon to be forgotten.

Brief summary about how it feels to have Anorexia Nervosa

An extract from my diary

Most of the time, even envisioning a life without being in the firm grip of anorexia seemed impossible. Perfection, however unattainable, seemed to be the one and only option. In order to quench that thirst, I watched my dress size drop to the point that I was affecting puberty and became a nineteen-year-old woman trapped in a ten-year-old girl's body. Before I left the front door each day, I made sure I was dressed with a fake smile to disguise the brewing cauldron of unhappiness — the only emotion that existed within me at the time — and to ensure that suspicions didn't arise about my deadly secret. My secret being my supposed best friend, anorexia.

Days passed, months went by and, in the blink of an eye, I found myself pleading at death's door, unable to string a sentence together or partake in anything without a wave of exhaustion hitting me each time. I was in denial that my body was giving up on me at such a young age. My days were counted, my heart was straining to pump blood around my body and every breath I took felt as though it could have been my last. The doctors stressed this to me countless times as I lay there in a hospital gown, strapped up to a heart monitor and drips from all directions, with cannulas placed anywhere, from top to bottom, depending on whether they were lucky enough to find a good vein. I was prodded and poked by nurses, even during the middle of the night, due to the long-standing risk of me falling into a coma at any moment. I was helped to use the bathroom and then was told off for standing up rather than using a wheelchair when I was fully capable of using my legs. I thought everyone was being overdramatic when I was perfectly fine, but I failed to realise I was deluded by the lies anorexia was whispering constantly into my ear.

It was hard. Harder than anything I've faced in the past, harder than I anticipated it to be and harder, surely, than any punishment implemented in the cruellest judiciary system, including a lifetime sentence. I found even getting out of bed was laborious in itself. Every meal was planned in advance and the number of steps to do each day was non-negotiable. I couldn't help but question what the point of waking up each morning was and I even contemplated whether my existence was just a waste of space. I convinced myself that the world would be a better place without me.

CHAPTER 2
The response of family and friends

I'm not entirely sure if my family were more in denial than I was. If I really think about it now, the answer would, surprisingly, be yes. This was evident any time the phrase "mentally unwell" or similar sprung up in conversation and was quickly diverted, ignored like it never happened or disregarded with something like, "Don't be silly; you don't know what mental health is."

Not only were they trying to get their heads around having to watch their daughter die in front of their eyes, but also the fact that they were completely helpless, which, frankly, is any parents' worst nightmare. As a parent, you are conditioned to protect your child from any setbacks or misfortunes that life throws at them. Unfortunately, there were no parenting guides nor support groups, nor any quantity of parenting experience that could have prepared them for the sheer pain and unbearable torment their child would experience in the grasp of the disorder.

At the beginning, the outbursts were mistakenly seen as natural repercussions of being a hormonal teenager, but then came the low self-esteem and overly seeking reassurance, which were momentarily addressed by an abundance of makeup, to the extent that I was unrecognisable. I became so wrapped up in chasing this distorted image of beauty that everything else, whether it was family time, friendships or education, became very insignificant. When faced with decision-making, reluctance and ambivalence was a common occurrence. My chirpy and resilient self – which didn't settle for anything less than perfect – was now engulfed by this demon. It accused me of being selfish and called me derogatory terms. Irrational fears around gaining weight arose. Living became that little bit harder. Thinking for myself became unmanageable and breathing was a battle.

Introduction to the available mental health services

The half-term break of February 2015 was a pivotal point in my life. Up until then, I was confined to either school or home, and was certainly not familiar with a life beyond the four walls of those two locations.

At the time, I was 15 years old. I still had paths to venture through, exams to complete, friendships to make and occasions to celebrate. But nothing could have prepared me for what I was about to hear. In hindsight, every grade was of miniscule importance, a heartbreak was definitely not the end of the world, and life does not revolve around the number of followers or likes you have on social media. Life was so much more than the bubble I was enclosed in, but sadly this is still the case for a lot of teenagers today. Everything I knew and loved dearly was cruelly snatched away from me. I could not piece together why my parents were in utter shock and so distraught at the sight of seeing their little girl in a hospital gown attached to a heart monitor. I just thought of it as parents being parents, worrying unnecessarily, as per usual. Not so long before, I had been up and about, running around like a hyperactive child, bursting with energy, eager to be the first one in class. I rugby-tackled anyone, regardless of whether they were six foot ten or a minion like me, just to get to the top of the queue for lunch, especially on my favourite fishy-fry days. By this point, I had used every excuse in the book for my secret not to be revealed. I had no more tears left to cry or a voice to advocate the struggle without seeming vain. My parents and the clinicians watched me like hawks in hospital, not a second to spare elsewhere. I was still baffled as to why, but there were more than 100 unanswered questions in my parents' mind, none of which were answered efficiently.

Fortunately, my friends and family were, and still are, one of my biggest assets. Distance never acted as a barrier to our friendship or family bond because I was lucky enough to have friends and family who were there for the laughs, light-hearted conversations and having my back, but they also became a shoulder to cry on, a therapist without the expenses, who would help me declutter my mind and put things into perspective and, above all, made me feel truly loved. Even when things were tough, they spurred me on and rushed to my aid whenever I needed it. I am eternally grateful for each and every one of you. Without you, I would not have become the person that I can proudly say that I am today. I am Gisel Josy and I am not 1 in 4. Anorexia will not steal any more of my precious years. It will not barricade any more windows of opportunities in front of me and, for once, I can see a future outside the four walls of a psychiatric ward.

Why me?

This is a question I still ask myself to this day. Sometimes I can answer it without a shadow of doubt, but other times I am in two minds and unable to reach a conclusion I am satisfied with.

As teenagers, we have a tendency to pick out our flaws and anything that is considered as wrong or unattractive with oneself. We heavily rely on other people's opinions and are lost in the pursuit of meeting unrealistic expectations imposed by society. Therefore, we struggle to accept praise or compliments without judgement and this trait is programmed to follow us throughout the rest of adulthood, if not tackled appropriately.

A common way of addressing this problem is keeping insecurities at bay and not allowing vulnerabilities to be exposed, as they're sometimes seen as a sign of weakness. This means we are immersed with the need to fit in and conform to the standards of those around us, and the desire to stand out and be unique has started to become uncommon.

In secondary school, a lot of what we learnt wasn't relevant to real life. How to say different pizza toppings in French, how to do Pythagoras' Theorem and how to read Shakespeare's poetry were covered in the curriculum, but, in my opinion, these were pointless pieces of information. Those who were considered as not being very intellectually bright – or book smart, as I refer to it – were already ruled out as failures before they set foot into the outside world. Education is slowly but surely detaching from its first and foremost objective, which is to be the breeding ground for growing well-rounded knowledge, developing own opinions and beliefs, and gaining an insight into the ever-changing world around us.

I was one of those students that many envied, because I was intellectually bright and got the top grades in class, but I pushed myself up and beyond my limits to do so. I wanted to make myself proud, as well as those around me – the cultural aspect of being Asian played a huge role in this, too. It wasn't the easiest of rides, to say the least, and I put immense pressure on myself to reach the top grades. Nothing short of the highest was good enough. These high expectations for myself spread within all aspects of my life, whether it was sports, arts and crafts or recreational activities. It also sculpted the start of my eating disorder. The thrill I received from losing weight was like no other. It gave me the sense of accomplishment that I craved. Being the thinnest was my only goal in life at the time... or so I believed.

Do you have to be an inpatient to recover? Otherwise I am not ill enough, right?

This is quite a misleading question as it's suggesting that becoming an inpatient is the only effective way to recover, as though you need justification to want to get better. This concept demonstrates the grasp that the eating disorder has on you. The vast majority of us don't wish for ill health. Our bodies are built to fend for themselves against any pathogens/ foreign bodies or undergo a healing mechanism (clotting and scab formation) when there is a wound and the hypothalamus helps regulate our body temperature. These reactions happen without a second thought, like reflex actions brought on by a stimulus, as our bodies are designed to live for long periods of time. This was apparent even in prehistoric times when there was the survival of the fittest. Without this, our bodies wouldn't be able to undergo essential life processes that ensure the existence of the human race in, say, 300 years' time. You would not find people hoping and doing everything in their means for a cold to turn into pneumonia, then for their lungs to collapse and eventually be at death's door. This shows how absurd and flawed the thinking is, but anorexia is such a deceptive illness, whereby sufferers are brainwashed and left with the remains of a distorted perspective of normality, unhelpful associations with food and disagreements that trigger unstable relationships. It leaves you with a lifetime of misery and isolation. Does this sound appealing? It not only feeds into the ED but also the stigma around evaluating the severity of a mental illness via physical symptoms, e.g. BMI. Doing so creates an effect that is similar to adding gasoline to a burning fire: it creates a bigger and more ferocious blaze. The issue is amplified and prolongs the steps taken towards real recovery.

What does being recovered entail? How do you envision recovery to be and why is it so hard?

If you define recovery only in terms of what is stated in an English dictionary, it would be easy to understand and the concept would exist without ambiguity or differences of opinion. Though this approach isn't realistic (because one's recovery is never parallel to another), we need to familiarise ourselves with the generic meaning of recovery as a starting point. It is "the act or process of returning to your normal state of health, mind or strength after an illness, injury, financial crisis and so on". In addition, when referring to rehabilitation after a significant mental health crisis such as Anorexia Nervosa, every effective treatment and recovery method is stemmed by a holistic approach. This ensures that the sufferer is equipped with the skills to initiate recovery, as follows:

1) A – Accept that there is a problem and be willing to take steps to move forward.
2) N – Never give up, even after falling countless times at the same hurdle.
3) O – Open your eyes to the sight of a world brimming with opportunities that anorexia had selfishly snatched away from you for so long.
4) R – Remember to utilise the incentives and support networks around you, whether it's family, friends, next-door-neighbours, your dog or even your teddy bear.
5) E – Enjoy the little things in life and create memories you can cherish forever, without being bounded by the restrictions placed by this illness.
6) X – eXperience and appreciate new beginnings. Don't let this illness hold you back anymore. Perfection is unattainable, hence why you should only strive to be a

better version of yourself from yesterday and nothing more.

7) I – Inform other sufferers and those dear to them of the lasting detrimental consequences that anorexia poses, which can overshadow any potential benefits it supposedly offers. Do not be ashamed to talk openly about mental health, while advocating the reasons to recover despite the hiccups on the way.

8) A – Acknowledge the fact that not everyone will understand the complexities or see the finer details of this illness, even the professionals (whose expertise comes down to a mere grade on a piece of paper and their ability to retain information from religiously reading stacks of textbooks and studies). Instead, welcome and appreciate those who have a desire to understand better and will do anything in their power to do so. Listen to those who have your best interests at heart. Be able to unravel and dismiss the lies that are said to you every time you stand in front of a mirror, so that this illness will not remain a hindrance for any longer.

Help me to understand – why is it so hard?

This question is very subjective, and I am not implying that this is the hardest battle to combat and nothing else is comparable to it, because there is no straightforward way of measuring the severity of an illness. In fact, the type and duration tells you very little, so you have to mainly rely upon the person affected, their situation and whether this difficulty causes such an impediment to their daily life that everything else becomes almost non-existent. It's similar to trying to complete a jigsaw puzzle that already has pieces that are misleading; they appear to fit and temporarily replace the actual missing piece, but they do not create the desired picture. This analogy is applicable to real life, as we are all so wrapped up in the fear of failure and faltering at the first hurdle that we compromise with the first satisfactory result. Surviving for the sake of getting by in life seems to be the new motto, which overrides the desire to live a fulfilling life.

This is why, again and again, anorexia manages to creep through in times of hardship and despondence. It becomes that jigsaw piece that doesn't quite fit, but will make do for the time being. The comfort, drive and reassurance each victim receives temporarily can actually strengthen anorexia's grip and means that it manifests into a hidden, soothing, yet deadly secret. So, those who have severe and enduring eating disorders find it hard to adjust to change and instead aim for a life that sustains anorexia.

This is because many are unable to comprehend the extent to which anorexia has a role in their life and why there would be such a desperate need for change. This lack of understanding is somewhat due to the feeling of shame imprinted by society regarding mental health, despite the fact it is all around us. All we need to do is open our eyes to it.

What is to blame if someone doesn't recover?

When a recovery is deemed a failure, the finger is usually pointed at the unbearable weight gain and the difficulty around reinstating food into a sufferer's life. However, if you are under the illusion that maintaining a good weight and a healthy diet are the only factors that need to be sorted to achieve a full recovery, I am sorry to burst your bubble. It's all well and good being able to reach a healthy weight, as it enables you to engage in everyday activities without the need to stop to catch your breath every ten minutes and, above all, your body starts to trust you. However, this becomes a waste when you are unable to keep the weight on; in fact, the continuous yo-yoing between gaining and losing weight can take an even bigger toll on your body. In addition, you begin to dread social interactions, and the things you used to find happiness in now come at a cost.

We are all too invested in the idea that a journey is about travelling from A to B to reach a destination without delay or inconvenience. Let's elaborate on this misconception with an example: if there was an aircraft travelling from Rome to Miami, you would have a rough idea of the expected journey time, how long boarding formalities would take and details about the airplane, terminal and check-in time.

However, these are all estimations and not a promised fact; indeed, there may well be a hold-up due to an unaccompanied bag at the airport, the airplane might not take off because of technical errors that mean your flight is suspended or turbulence might cause disruptions when the plane is about to land. However, we don't always intend for delays or blips to happen, which would heighten anxiety and cause further unexpected issues to arise. If all was well, it would be a smooth plane ride with staff being efficient and surpassing your expectations to make your journey comfortable. This is similar to recovery; we need to find the fine balance between not getting stuck in a yo-yoing state, but expect to find bumps along the way and utilise that to create a successful recovery overall.

We do not always have to anticipate the worst possible situation, because it might not occur that time around. It is about simply weighing up both the good and the bad, as well as acknowledging that real-life situations don't go as planned all of the time. If expectations always became reality, we would not be able to appreciate the little things that we take for granted; life would have a predictable, clichéd fairy tale ending; and you would not be able to build resilience and have the ability to keep going in spite of difficulties. Blips should not be seen as setbacks, but rather an opportunity for you to grow and become a better version of yourself. That is what anorexia recovery is all about.

What to expect when your child has an eating disorder

First of all, it is important to become familiar with what the term CAMHS means. CAMHS stands for Child and Adolescent Mental Health Services (NHS), which supports those with behavioural, emotional or psychological problems that interrupt their social lives, schooling, milestones and family life. It is vital to know not only what it stands for, but who is able to seek help with the service, as well as how decisions are made in regards to what treatment is offered (depending on whether it's suitable for your presentation and the setting at which this will take place, either in the community (outpatients or day care) or as an inpatient. This includes those who are critically underweight or those whose physical/mental health is so compromised that intensive and immediate treatment from a general hospital is required due to the risk of fatality. For many, CAMHS is a term that is unheard of, unless it's stumbled upon because you, a loved one, a peer or a friend is under their treatment or because your profession is closely related to mental health. Looking back, I was clueless about this condition and undermined the major impact it would have on my life until that label became undetachable. My parents were helpless, for once; it was a field that they had no experience in.

Many families have shared similar experiences, because anorexia is wrongly portrayed as self-inflicted and a consequence of vanity. In actual fact, it stems from underlying insecurities provoked by less favourable environmental changes. Within our human instinct, the element of control is key and this is the difference between drifting passively through life for the sake of others or taking ownership of every action and creating a life that is unique to you. For some, when this element of control is challenged and you are not equipped with strategies or skills that can effectively combat this, it can lead to an unintentional domino effect, which, in turn, can contribute to the emergence of an eating disorder.

The main characteristics of Anorexia Nervosa include irrational fears and beliefs related to life's necessities, such as food and water. It is an illness with many deceiving faces; any way you turn, you are confronted with something new. Due to these complexities, there is no accurate definition or description that depicts what the diagnosis of anorexia entails for each sufferer, as the manifestations can vary greatly. This means that there is always a new piece of information or revelation that can help those who have years of experience and have the theoretical knowledge – i.e. psychiatrists, to receive a more well-rounded understanding beyond the paragraphs in a textbook and instigate a holistic approach that is tailored for each patient's needs.

The recovery process is similar to peeling an onion with never-ending layers. There will be tears on the way to achieving the desired end result (a peeled onion), but its never-ending layers will take you by surprise and are never quite the same as the one before. The truth of the matter is that there is no one who has infinite knowledge about this illness and there is no specific treatment method or facility that will guarantee recovery for all suffering. This is a disconcerting thought for sufferers and their loved ones, but it is reality, whether in the workplace, at social gatherings, in school and even the home environment. There is no 'perfect' solution. Despite this, recovery is what you make of it; enforcing treatment upon a sectioned patient in order for them to reach a healthy weight can work for some, but it is far from effective for many and not a long-term fix, in my opinion.

Without a shadow of a doubt, weight restoration is a key component to recovery, but it is not the deciding factor. Many presume that reaching a healthy weight equates to a full recovery, because, surely, if you are not emaciated and at death's door, you are not anorexic? I cannot stress enough the importance of society recognising that Anorexia Nervosa is a mental disorder, which displays symptoms that can need immediate medical attention. For example, hypoglycemia (low blood sugars) and hypotension (low blood pressure) and so on are the results of extreme starvation and neglecting the body. Our bodies are intricately designed to endure pain while minimising the risk of infection; they repair and protect as quickly as possible and strive to function as a full, working body. The after-effects of an enduring eating disorder might not be immediately apparent, but detrimental consequences invisible to the naked eye can exist, such as some forms of osteopenia or osteoporosis, which increases the risk of fractures or breaks, a loss of normal menstruation in women, difficulties conceiving or even infertility, and many more.

It is crucial that you do not stop halfway as you peel through the layers, because the end goal is within reaching distance. One of the key reasons my parents found it hard to get their heads around the disorder was the lack of understanding and awareness, and therefore an inability to accept help from mental health services due to overriding feelings of shamefulness. It has been found that early intervention is crucial and can be make-or-break for a successful recovery with minimal or no detrimental consequences. It does not certify recovery, but it puts you in the best possible position for it to take place. If in any doubt, GPs or a responsible clinician should be the first point of call. On the other hand, we need to acknowledge the fact that in recent years there has been a shift in the way we approach the topic of mental health due to media exposure, more of the population recognising their diagnosis or acts of philanthropy. We have come such a long way from the 12th-13th centuries where self-starvation for women was seen as a religious practice and a way of showing their devotion to God, to being recognised as part of the DSM-III (Diagnostic and Statistical Manual of Mental Health Disorders) in the 1980's.

Do not feel alarmed if your child starts displaying these symptoms, because Anorexia Nervosa is not solely responsible. It could be down to various other factors, some of which correlate with fluctuations in hormone levels (which is very common during puberty). It could also be linked to peer pressure or copying celebrities, which teenagers, in particular, have a tendency to do. A person should seek help as soon as possible if there are changes not only in physical appearance, but mood and health. Help should also be sought if there is an increase in irrational fears around weight gain and food, and these fears are persistent for an extensive period of time and notably impact life in a negative manner.

All my parents did was cling onto their little girl with all their might in the hope that one day she would be released from the grasp of anorexia and be able to have a life she had always envisioned. However, she was slowly but surely slipping away and all they could do was helplessly watch it happen in front of their eyes.

The transition between CAMHS and adult services

Once it's apparent that community treatment is either not suitable for the presenting condition or outpatients have failed to tackle the issue effectively, even after what seemed to be an adequate period of time – and this can also mean that some may have deteriorated to the point admission is no longer negotiable – then another care option will be considered. This isn't a decision that is taken lightly; it requires a lot of thought and the team will collaboratively weigh up the pros and cons and come to a collective decision in the patient's best interest. The aim is to provide the most appropriate care, which will steer a patient in the direction of recovery.

I have experienced both being a patient within CAMHS and as an adult, and I can tell you that it is a whole new ball game when you set foot into adult services. There is no anchor to hold you in place and no driving force to keep you going. Ultimately, the initiative has to come from you. As an adult, you have more say in your treatment than ever before.

For some, this is the time to showcase a true determination to get better independently, with the aid of health clinicians in the background; while others become trapped in a vicious cycle of quasi-recovery that inhibits them from leading their fullest lives, since there is no one to administer boundaries until absolutely necessary. Anorexia is a manipulative illness whereby the patient will do anything to cut corners and find ways out of doing what is needed to get better, so just imagine combining that with the freedom that is present in adult services.

My intention is not to scare you into thinking that adult services won't provide any help, because they most certainly will. However, speaking from experience, if you want to achieve a better life for yourself, the willpower and driving force needs to come from you. No one can force that on you. All you can do is use your support network, listen to what the health professionals say and be concordant with your treatment plan.

What it means to not be the 'stereotypical' anorexic

Let's all close our eyes and picture a stereotypical anorexic. It's likely that you have imagined an emaciated size zero catwalk model in her early adult years, Caucasian, flaunting her "desirable" skeletal figure, which more or less resonates the remains of a dead body. There's so much more to this life-threatening illness that does exist beyond the red carpet, magazine covers and social media feeds. It is practically at every corner we turn: children's playgrounds have become the breeding ground for insecurities; Botox and surgical clinics are now festered with clients; prom has become a beauty pageant rather than mirroring the end of a chapter in your life that ought to be celebrated; and cosmetic sales have rocketed in efforts to correct your "imperfections or flaws", so that you resemble the "ideal body" as closely as possible.

We are all deeply entrenched in the idea of weight loss equating to a more "attractive" version of ourselves, in the desire to get society's approval. But what about when your gaunt face becomes as pale as the clouds; patches of bald accompanied by straggly lifeless hair that is as fine as the bristles on an overused toothbrush appear; and your breath reeks to the point that the pungent smell of sewage is more tolerable? These are only a handful of the untold truths about living with anorexia, excluding the devastating health complications it can induce, the derogatory thoughts that haunt you each day, distancing yourself from any love or affection because of the belief of inadequacy and worthlessness, and feeling constantly dissatisfied with your body. Every pound lost, every dress size dropped and every inch of your waist shed is another smile wiped off your face; the twinkle in your eye is nowhere to be seen and with it goes even the desire to wake up the next morning. The genuineness in your laugh is no longer there and you waste away ruminating about the next meal, the next calorie you ought to burn and the next number you strive to be. All these adverse consequences remain hidden and we are tormented by social media posts or advertisements – particularly at the beginning of each year, with the emphasis on a "new year, new me" approach to compensate for the "overindulgence" of the festive period. Food is categorised as either "naughty" or "sin-free". If there are foods considered to have a "high" fat content, contain too many unnecessary calories or a high sugar content, it is automatically classed as "naughty", as it can tamper with your weight loss and makes you more prone to experiencing the opposite effect (supposedly). However, I believe this approach is very misleading and can increase the likelihood for an unhealthy relationship between you and food. You thought relationships with humans were tricky enough, but you just started a whole new board game!

As soon as a child steps foot into school, they are made aware of the importance of a balanced diet in an effort to combat child obesity, which can carry on through to adulthood if left untreated. This creates future health problems whereby resources are stretched and expenses for the NHS soars. Meanwhile, we fail to recognise how essential these foods are within our diet and how excluding them means depriving our bodies of the nutrients required for healthy functioning. This is counteracting your intention to lead a healthy lifestyle and can potentially cause increased appetite or unbearable cravings, which can have a detrimental effect on your diet and, more importantly, on how you go about your day-to-day life.

For instance, dietary fats are needed within our bodies for the absorption of vitamins, supporting cell growth and ensuring that the body has sufficient energy to last the day. Calories are wrongly accused of being the main culprit for weight gain, and high calorie foods are seen as a no-go zone, especially during a diet, when, in actual fact, a calorie is simply a unit that is used to measure energy. Calories are essential for the survival of the human race; without it, we would be unable to undergo basic life processes, such as respiration and digestion. Brain metabolism alone requires 20 per cent of our daily calorie intake and regardless of whether you are an athlete that trains six hours a day, a hyperactive five-year-old who has just started school or someone on a ventilator attached to a life support machine, everyone needs sufficient calories.

Diets occur across all seasons. After Easter and demolishing six Lindt bunnies in one sitting, you soon find yourself surrounded by the new summer craze of the "beach body". This not only takes the fun out of summer, but it leaves you ambivalent about going out and enjoying the sun, due to the overwhelming fear of being judged or criticised by strangers. Why do men need a six pack, a toned physique, broad shoulders and bulky arms to justify embracing the sunshine while it lasts? Do women need a perky bum, small waist, a toned body and the perfect hourglass figure to be comfortable wearing a bikini in the scorching heat? The answer is no. Most of the world is apparently fixated on weight loss as a solution to all of life's problems or as a convenient way of diverting your attention from the actual problems. We need to reinstate our priorities in life, firstly by helping to eradicate some of the vast array of pointless phrases we use in this day and age, such as, "New year, new me," "Get that beach body" and "Do you even lift, bro?"

The idea of the stereotypical anorexic stems from the media and what society has ingrained in our heads for so long. Did the dieting culture lead to anorexia or is it vice versa? It seems to be the case of finding whether the chicken or egg came first, but either way they are both apparent and an issue that needs to be resolved, because both take equal precedence. That is not to say dieting is always a bad thing because for some it is necessary and beneficial to their wellbeing if done in a controlled, healthy manner with the involvement of a health professional.

Dual diagnosis of BPD and Anorexia Nervosa

I am going to talk about this from my own experience of having a dual diagnosis of borderline personality disorder (BPD) and Anorexia Nervosa. It is worth noting that people with BPD have a greater prevalence of eating disorders than people in the general population. A study showed that 21.7 per cent of patients with BPD met criteria for Anorexia Nervosa – and why is that you ask? A possible explanation could be that these diagnoses share a common risk factor: they are both linked to invalidating factors such as a history of childhood trauma or abuse, which elevates the likelihood for BPD and eating disorders to emerge. Also, the symptoms of BPD, such as impulsivity and urges to self-harm, may lead to problematic eating patterns as a coping mechanism or a form of self-neglect, and can overtime establish an eating disorder within the patient. Conversely, it can work the opposite way around: an eating disorder or engaging in those disordered eating behaviours may lead to experiences of stress due to hospitalisation, difficult family dynamics and shame, which, in turn, may trigger BPD in someone with a genetic vulnerability or a predisposition for the disorder.

Dear 12-year-old Gisel,

I know things are extremely hard at the moment, my darling – in fact, that may well be an understatement. It feels like your fate was doomed since the day you started to comprehend things and develop an opinion of your own. There is no reasonable justification or excuse that can account for the torture you endure every day, hour, minute, second that goes by and in every breath you take. But please, however painful it may be to hear, you need to realise that you are wrong for once — no, that voice inside your head that questions your worth and planted a false sense of accomplishment with every pound you lose and the days you waste away is wrong. I want you to leave the ego-centred, stubborn, hard-to-please armour behind, Gisel, because you are treading in murky waters here and those around you are tiptoeing quietly to not wake the beast brewing inside you. Your parents are scared of losing their little girl, who was nothing short of perfect to them. They refuse to raise their head high in society because of the foreboding accusatory looks from others. They condemn their efforts as failings in being good parents and wake up startled each night in fear that there may be no tomorrow for their only daughter.

We tend to associate mourning with a period of bereavement or grief for the loss of a loved one and the longing desire to see them one more time, while hopelessly attempting to fill that void in your life. These are healthy, normal reactions to experience during difficult periods in one's life, but similar feelings can be triggered for those helplessly watching their child, sibling, partner or loved one digging their own grave in front of their own eyes, because this illness is nothing but selfish, sparing no mercy for those who fall victim. The elation provided by weight loss is often temporary and the initial benefits usually subside over time, especially after excessive dieting and the adoption of unhelpful compensatory behaviours such as overexercise, purging etc.

Before you realise, you will find yourself in the firm grip of anorexia, unable to let go or fathom a thought about life without it. It will destroy your life in every aspect. I know you are desperately trying to seek some sort of love and affection, which seems impossible at the moment. You want to be acknowledged and reassured that your struggles are not going to get the better of you. Your existence, for the time being, seems overlooked. Your life is on pause and there are other things in the forefront of everyone's minds. This is hard for you, little 12-year-old Gisel, who wishes to be the centre of attention like any other little child of your age, receiving comments such as, "She's so cute" or "Good job". Is that too much to ask from a twelve-year-old?

The reality is that this illness gifts you with nothing other than a lifetime of misfortune and torn relationships, which will never be replaced by the so-called "benefits" that anorexia offers – an emaciated body covered in lanugo hair, the inability to go up a flight of stairs without passing out and the struggle to engage in conversation.

Resisting the temptation to give in to the crippling voice inside your head seems like the easiest and most logical route, but for those with anorexia it sounds absolutely absurd. Patient cooperation throughout the recovery process is, primarily, the make-or-break of a full recovery, regardless of how much you enforce it against their will through a section, CTO or hospitalisation. You need to take the initiative to start recovery. There may not be a light bulb moment or a sense of readiness, but you need to stop holding back and take the plunge – otherwise, as each day passes, it will only get harder to manage. Eventually, you'll find resilience to overcome obstacles, especially ones you've faltered at again and again, and determination to prove doubters wrong. You deserve to pat yourself on the back when you start regaining control of your life.

In order to do so, we need to broaden our understanding of how this illness comes about for each individual and why some are able to make, what's known as, a "full" recovery, why others constantly switch between the two states (recovery and relapse) and, unfortunately, why many fall victim to the illness or only just survive it. Please choose wisely, Gisel. Your whole life is ahead of you, remember!

It is clear to see that the illness stems from underlying insecurities, so nourishing a sufferer by what is mistakenly depicted as their worst enemy (food) is all well and good. However, there are other aspects that require just as much attention or more, such as weight restoration to optimise healthy body functioning and being able to oppose delusional beliefs that can do more harm than good. Moreover, ensuring that each patient is equipped with sufficient, transferable skills that can keep them out of hospital after leaving and providing the stepping stones for them to lead a more normal, carefree life. I have found that many hospitals are caught up in providing immediate and attentive care for the visible physical health complications – which is only a minor symptom or *by-product of the infinite struggles faced – but that is only one side of this disorder. It undermines the overwhelming grief your head gives you after each meal and the isolated life you begin to lead in your early developmental years: the time in your life where socialisation and finding your feet are arguably the most major components. So, rather than jumping blindly into the option of inpatient, give the outpatient treatment a go, knowing that the possibility of relapse is around the corner.*

This brings me back to the question, Gisel, as to why you would jeopardise reaching the heights you aspire to reach, or the dreams you believe will come true? For what, anorexia? Like most children with an Asian background, education is seen as the only key to success and a resource that opens many doors. However, if you cannot foresee a future (in the short-term) without this illness, do not be disheartened because it is not the end of the road. Yes, prevention is the best cure, but everything happens for a reason and it has made you the person you are today.

You are living proof that there is hope. You are not claiming to be recovered because that will tarnish the true meaning of recovery and the sheer hard work that makes it a reality. I picture it as a fight where the ultimate prize is regaining what was rightfully yours in the first place, your life, otherwise you fall into the firm grips of anorexia, which is equivalent to a slow, painful death.

Why weight restoration doesn't necessarily equate to full recovery

Society is under the illusion that anorexia recovery involves weight restoration and weight restoration alone. How close you are to a healthy weight is often mistaken as the factor that determines how far along someone is in their recovery. However, a simple numerical value does in no way indicate the sufferer's mental stability and should only be seen as progression in terms of physical health. Yet again, I cannot emphasise enough that Anorexia Nervosa is a mental illness that cannot be resolved with weight gain alone – if that was the case, it would not have the highest mortality rate of all mental health conditions. Not everyone with anorexia is ghastly pale, thin and at death's door. The weight loss is the aftermath; some see it as the most apparent symptom of this very misunderstood illness, therefore it is treated before introducing therapy.

Studies have shown that our brain's cognitive ability, awareness and processing does improve significantly with increased nutritional intake and those who are physically compromised cannot optimise the therapy provided to aid their recovery efficiently. This applies not only for us humans, but all living organisms, vehicles and other electronic devices that require food, fuel or batteries to run. You wouldn't set off on a seven-hour car journey with little to no fuel in the tank, so why treat your body any differently?

Reaching and maintaining a healthy weight is imperative for those aiming for a full recovery, but it is not the be-all and end-all. It is only a small component within a still very much misunderstood illness, which never fails to astonish even the most experienced clinicians. Each case that falls under the umbrella term of anorexia is similar, but so different. Many encounter different struggles, have various triggers and can unveil different perplexities that ought to be treated with an individualised and holistic approach.

What we need to remember is that it is a mental illness and it can unfold in various ways, so keeping the door ajar for anorexia to creep back in when least expected only heightens the intensity of any struggles. This position is probably harder than committing to recovery wholeheartedly or choosing to sustain a life with anorexia. Some describe it as having one foot out and one foot in, and this level of uncertainty means it is not unusual for sufferers to have a depleted quality of life and find themselves constantly between home and hospital. The thing to remember is that relapses are not failings on yours or your family's part, because every step back or falling into what I call a 'lapse' only builds resilience, gives you a better insight of your struggles at the time and, more importantly, allows that flicker of hope within you to ignite a burning flame that doesn't admit defeat easily. I've had what I believed were light bulb moments in which recovery seemed more than an unattainable hypothetical dream. It was feasible and I could foresee a life where anorexia didn't have the power to taunt me again. I was indestructible for once – or so I thought.

But I failed to realise that recovery is not all about actively trying to do things perfectly nor putting immense pressure on oneself to forcefully drain the voice in your head. It is the ability to recognise the voice inside your head, despite how strong or quiet it may seem, and to willingly seek support to dampen it and share the burden to ensure that your road to recovery progresses. It is normal to feel alone in this battle. It is draining – mentally and physically – but if your drive to get better is strong enough, nothing can overpower this.

There were several occasions where the taste of freedom was brutally snatched from me by anorexia. I thought I had learned my lesson after spending countless birthdays in hospital. I found myself hysterically crying in disgust and cursing it because of what it had done, but nevertheless I ran back to it. For what? I asked myself again and again. I am still searching for that answer, but am in no doubt that I will find the strength to overcome this battle, once and for all.

EXAMPLE DAY AS AN INPATIENT IN AN EATING DISORDERS UNIT (EDU)

In hospital, the days drag into what seems like a lifetime. Each hour is pretty much the same, and every minute is more unbearable and tedious than sitting an A level maths exam. I often find myself watching the clock for the next meal, the next time I can go on my walk, the time when the rest period would be over and I can get my ass off this bloody chair, which probably has my bum cheeks imprinted in it by now. Thinking about every dreaded meal and sitting down all of the time is tortuous.

I wouldn't wish this fear on anybody and it baffles me even now. I am not surprised that it doesn't make much sense to someone who hasn't experienced or come across an eating disorder before. The screams from ng feeds bellowing down the corridor in broad daylight still rings in my ears. I can feel the tube piercing my nasal passage and every limb in my body being pinned down by staff to aid the feed.

During my time in hospital, I realised it's easier for clinicians to address the physical complications that come hand in hand in with anorexia than anything else. Any cracks on the surface usually go untouched; usually the aim is to restore weight to a sustainable level and nothing more. It is also very common to find patients on an extensive waiting list for treatment, and immediate, attentive care is only considered when someone is face-to-face with death.

This is similar to covering up potholes without dealing with the underlying cracks. This can result in all of the hard work that went into fixing the potholes going to waste and the problem continues to arise again and again. That is why we see so many "revolving door" patients time and time again. Every time it happens, I question whether I will be next.

Why might loved ones find it so hard to accept this diagnosis?

It is hard to promise certainty for someone when you are not sure what the future holds for them. This is very apparent during ED recovery, especially when you are trying to understand and comprehend the hardships that someone dear to you has to endure on a daily basis, with your hands tied to your back as you watch helplessly. The last thing you should do is give false promises to anyone, let alone someone struggling with an illness that has encroached on every aspect of their life and made it impossible for them to integrate back into normality – or whatever is perceived as normality. The only thing remaining is a shell of a person or, in extreme cases, just a name on a gravestone. Another common unhelpful behaviour of many parents, carers or loved ones is the need to unintentionally reinforce expectations on the person as a way of reassurance or signifying that you believe in them. This is not to say that relaying your views or opinions on a matter, especially when someone is seeking your advice or asking for an alternative perspective, is unacceptable. It is, in fact, a perfectly healthy response. However, there is a fine line between that and reciting a person's capabilities to them – or, more accurately, what you believe their capabilities to be

– and dismissing the severity of their struggles with "There are people who are worse off than you are." I understand that in most cases this would initially come from a place of compassion and genuine care, but there is a strong likelihood that many may start to internalise their struggles due to this and therefore avoid accessing help sooner because of feeling unworthy. This lack of early intervention can be the make or break for someone's recovery and the duration for which they sustain this illness. It is not a consolation, as we are under no illusion that our struggles outweigh anyone else's, but we are all still desperately in need of help, just like anyone with a physical impairment.

Expected grades or achievements in school or careers is very different from imposing impractical expectations on your child to recover (as soon as possible). If it was so easy, we wouldn't have extended waiting lists for an eating disorder inpatient bed and it wouldn't be such an enduring illness, killing so many unfortunate souls from as young as eight to as old as sixty plus. Parents, in particular, tend to seek out the positives and reinforce the capabilities of their children so as to reassure them that they do not need to feel as though they are fighting alone. For some, this acts as an incentive to work towards a goal, especially for those who are very much goal-oriented.

On the contrary to this is the overwhelming pressure this would place on the child/sufferer. Instead of restoring hope, they are burdened with expectations that they may not achieve straightaway, which makes them feel like a failure, further reinforcing derogatory thoughts.

The truth of the matter is that you cannot control someone else's response or reaction to a deed you've done. There is no need to place the blame on anyone or any individual thing, because this illness arises due to an accumulation of things, some of which are completely out of our control. Regardless of how perfect the treatment plan, support network and facilities, it ultimately comes down to how willing you are to let go and take the plunge – or whether you want to remain sitting on the fence because of the fear of failure, so continuing down the same path anorexia guides you down seems to be the "wisest" and "safest" option.

What is loneliness and why is it predominant during times of struggle?

Loneliness is more than just a feeling; it's a void in your life that is irreplaceable. Being among a crowd of people doesn't alleviate the pain. I am not blind to the fact that I am gifted with a loving family, one which I truly do not deserve. Instead, it is having the knowledge that the world has tarnished my ability to put any trust in people or even within myself, which is a frightening thought. This horrid illness reminds me every minute that I am not alone, because loneliness will always keep me company. I am not asking for an apology nor do I wish to hear any more meaningless words. A meaningful silence will do. There is no worse feeling than not being able to call anyone for help when you need it the most, nor having a shoulder to cry on or an ear to listen, in order to let off some steam.

I found greater companionship in solitude than in forced conversations with others, because at least I knew what I was confronting and I couldn't be disappointed. This stems from the belief that my existence is a waste of space. I am nothing but a nuisance to my friends and an utter disappointment to my family, so why would I live in a world where I clearly don't belong? This is the question that goes around and around in my head a million times and more each day.

But that is not to say they've broken my trust completely; they would have only done so if they'd been able to earn it in the first place – which many don't bother trying – others get tired of chipping down the armour halfway through, which is understandable and the minority who managed to persevere will always have a special place in my heart. In my eyes, any suspect is innocent until they are proven guilty, because we can't jump to conclusions straight away otherwise it's not an accurate or fair representation of the person and I believe in second chances to an extent.

On top of spending my teenage years and beyond trapped within the four walls of a psychiatric hospital, I was detained under the mental health act, which stripped me of any last remaining freedom and rights at the tender age of 15. I was then injected every time I was denounced as "too far gone" to be dealt with or even just as a precaution before any form of interaction with me, as though I was some sort of feral animal. It went against every law or regulation guideline, but this didn't deter them from doing it anyway. For some, me included, it became a daily occurrence. This situation can be best described as exploiting power and authority to diminish any speck of rights that a vulnerable patient has on the basis of a "lack of mental capacity". This doesn't always directly correlate with the mental health act and the two different matters need to be assessed separately. Your mental state can influence your mental capacity, but this should be reviewed every day, every time an incident occurs or during the build-up before something happens. It should not happen after the first six months of being on a Section 3, as you'll find the multidisciplinary team (MDT) manically trying to collate every past report and evidence to come to a conclusion on whether the section will be continued or rescinded. This is not only stressful for the professionals working tirelessly to meet deadlines, but also the patients, eagerly awaiting their fate.

I was tube-fed against my will and pinned to a chair with staff members holding down every limb and ligament in my body (similar to how a criminal posing a threat would be treated). In response, all I could do was wail, cry and scream until I had no voice to spare. However, before you jump to conclusions and decide that all inpatient settings are similar to the ones described above, I want you to know that this is only MY account of MY journey through hell, where rock bottoms were a typical occurrence and hating anyone who went against whatever my anorexia told me. To me, they were the "bad guys" or villains.

My mind was so deluded at the time that I couldn't process the vital piece of information that they were only doing all of this for my health's sake, to keep me adequately nourished and, simply, alive and breathing. Not because they found satisfaction in restraining me nor pleasure in seeing me well up with tears each time.

I vividly remember the time I was segregated into a room for months on end. The only glimpses of sunlight I saw were during the trips to A&E in a blue-lighted ambulance. But then I was told that my family – who had travelled almost halfway across the country in order to see me – were not allowed to come in. It was disheartening and frustrating for all of us. It wasn't a period of time in my life that I would want to relive. It is a past I am slowly trying to erase and, above all, an identity that I am trying to detach myself from because that is not me any longer. It was a manifestation of my illness that faked every smile and gave me false hope any time I put myself through torture. I don't want that to become my identity. I don't want the rest of the world to see me in that light. I have a name, a personality, a history beyond this and attributes that can take me far, if I give life a good go. I am not my illness. I am who I am. **I am Gisel Josy.**

What is the point of all of this?

Sorry for the slight negativity within this chapter, but this is the harsh, raw reality of living with a mental illness, never mind numerous disorders that don't have a magical cure and can make you suffer until you have no energy but to falter. Being an inpatient can have its negatives as well as positives: it is very much individualised on what you have to contend with in your journey to recovery. Like any form of treatment, it works the first time around for some, others need a few more attempts and some, unfortunately, end up becoming what is known as a revolving door patient. The choice is yours. Your willpower will carry you forward onto better things. It will allow you to let go of the grip that anorexia has on you and instead show you a world that has real opportunities, which will bring nothing but the best out of you. This means taking chances, trusting strangers by accepting that they have your best interests at heart and not letting one glitch set you back completely. There is no harder battle that requires more perseverance, determination and resilience than this one, so it will take a lot out of you – much more than expected at first. However, slowly but surely, each meal becomes less torturous, attending sociable occasions involving food becomes pleasurable, and even the little things like sharing a McNuggets box with a friend is no longer a daunting task that you try to avoid with an array of excuses, ready-made to be dished out each time.

You will no longer have that demon sitting on your shoulder. People will realise that it is so much more than starving for attention. You will be far from that "fussy child" who is overly particular with food. It's similar to wearing a mask that was disguising who you truly were and which tainted your perception of the world around you. Now, however, you will be set free, but only if you allow yourself to be.

An angel in disguise

This section is going to be dedicated to a very special woman, who was a part of my life for so long and never failed to put a smile on my face whenever I was lucky enough to see her. The section only shows a snippet of the incredible, strong-willed lady she was and still is. I could have easily written a book about her, but instead I had to compromise with just a section.

She was an advocate for those who could not be heard. She was the best therapist, but without the unnecessary expenses and hassle. Moreover, she spoke to us like we were people with aspirations, lives and attachments no different to anyone else. When she was on shift, there was no feeling of superiority or hierarchy between staff and patients. She was a mother figure, respected not only by us but by all of her colleagues, too.

She treated us with the utmost respect, love and compassion, the kind a mother would display to her children. Her advice was worth more than gold dust; she had abundant knowledge that enlightened each and every staff member that came through those doors for the first time. She reminded each one of us of how strong we were, even when giving up might seem like the easiest option. I could go on and on about her, because she was a miraculous lady that changed many lives, including mine. She had a healing power that reminded me of Jesus, cleansing the lepers of sickness.

She cannot be fairly credited in a couple of paragraphs, but the thing I love most about her was her genuineness and realism even when things were not 100 per cent or even 50 per cent. She was willing to share our burden, wipe our tears away and give us a pat on the back for trying our best. My only wish now is that I could have done the same for her and eased that little bit of pressure and stress off her, so that her hardships didn't seem as unbearable and didn't take as much of a toll on her wellbeing.

My anxiety was climbing the roof at this point; my fear became incomprehensible and in my head I was juggling an infinite amount of thoughts and numbers. Everything else got lost in the mix. Equally, this meant that I didn't realise time was ticking on and the world was still moving by, despite my life being on pause. All I seemed to care about was trying to work out the number of calories in front of me and how many steps I would need to do to compensate for it. Then, all of a sudden, my guardian angel swooped in and rescued me from this torment with a reassuring smile and a nod. This was enough for my anxieties to be put at bay, so that my struggles did not get the better of me. Anorexia might still have been present at that point, but that one is still a win in my eyes and spurred me on to do better next time around.

In the depths of my eating disorder, envisioning a life without it seemed impossible. My head was packed with numbers, derogatory terms, conflicting views and intrusive thoughts, and there was very little space for anything else. I was unable to hold a conversation for very long as I would always lose my train of thought and easily disengage if the topic didn't revolve around food or weight. Funnily enough, I remember muttering to myself, "Finally! Your maths skills are being put to use!" after religiously reciting the calories of each component of the meal in front of me. I convinced myself that the two scoops of vegan mash equated to a staggering 200kcal, at least, although deep down I knew it was just water and a bit of boiled potatoes. To put my mind at ease, I added another 50kcal as they are bound to be coated in oil. Everything supposedly tastes "better" with oil when, in actual fact, it is just a waste of calories and a marketing scam to make you fat. "Don't be a greedy pig and indulge in anymore, because you do not deserve it!"

It is hardly surprising that I was unable to keep up with a conversation regardless of my interest in it. My mind was far too occupied with disordered thoughts, which inevitably meant there was no room for anything else and secondly that everything else was deemed unimportant or secondary. When you are in such a dark hole, you forget that time is still ticking by and the Earth is still moving around its axis, but we can no longer see that only a portion of your life is made up of your struggles; instead, the struggles make up your entire life, which should not be the case.

This special lady acted as the little voice inside my head that prompted me to carry on despite the ongoing struggles. She gave me comfort and reassurance when I needed it most and that is why I am eternally grateful for her involvement. It restores my faith in humanity and shows that there is still some good in the world. It demonstrates that regardless of your title or position, a desirable attribute to have is to stay true to yourself and not sculpt a false image to suit a role. There is a clear difference between those who are purely working for a little bit of extra money in their pockets, compared to those who genuinely care and are doing it so they can have a positive impact on a patient's life. Not only was this lady a perfect example of this, she demonstrated that there is no harm in admitting you are in the wrong, when you truly know that you are. This is easily mistaken for naivety, when, in actual fact, it shows great maturity and the ability to take ownership of your actions, while being willing to initiate a change for the better without ego becoming a barrier. These were only a small selection of her most admirable qualities, which helped her succeed in her career and helped her to grow as an individual, looked up to and loved by so many.

But every time she shed a tear of despair, my heart ached. I could see the vulnerability in her eyes and the weakness engulfing her body as each day passed, but her spirit remained untampered. Technically speaking, I was just another patient detained under the mental health act who was reluctant to ask for help and resistive to treatment. Such a case was a common occurrence, but this did not deter her from making a laudable effort in getting to know each one of us as individuals. This is key for recovery, so that it is not just a fragment of our hopeful imagination or a hypothetical situation. The outside world will not know us for our diagnosis, but as the person we make ourselves out to be. Friends stem from compatible personalities/ interests and the family unit becomes one due to rebuilding trust.

She swooped in like my guardian angel, carried me when I was too tired to walk, held me close when I felt alone and told me that she loved me every single day. She very much resembled an angel to me and, without a doubt, she was a ray of sunshine to the entire ward. Without her, the ward would be disjointed and a great big mess. She was the missing piece that reminded us it would be okay and that tomorrow was another day.

Those who loved me...

Those who became friends with me and not my ED, stood by me.

Those who valued my presence although we were miles apart for countless months, stood by me.

Those who appreciated me for who I was and not for who I could be, stood by me.

Those who refused to give up on me, despite being ruled off as a lost cause time and time again, still stood by me.

You will encounter many passers-by during your journey: some who made a substantial difference at a particular pitstop and others who are just a familiar name without a face. The ones who made the effort to be at your side when you needed them most, the ones who received you with open arms after every apology and the ones who acknowledged you for the person you are today, they are the people in your life that really and truly matter.

Those three special words, 'I love you', don't need to be recited in every conversation with your special people, because you know them well enough and they know you well enough to know.

Love is an emotion – a feeling of affection like no other.

However, like many, I am beginning to doubt how accurate this definition really is. For example, if you take a look at text messages nowadays, the words 'I love you' are thrown around so easily. You even hear it in conversations where the topic of love is completely irrelevant. Valentine's Day cards seem to be incomplete if these three words aren't plastered on them. Normally, a word that is used out of context is said to be grammatically incorrect and a word that is overused is considered as a cliché. It's quite baffling that 'I love you' fits into both of these categories, but we do not hesitate to use it again and again. In some cases, 'I love you' is just a meaningless phrase, which can even be abbreviated to 'ily'. If a person can't be bothered to type more than those three letters on a keypad or click on an emoji, is that what you call love? The answer is no.

It's hardly surprising that the people I thought loved me just sat in the background, watching, as I crumbled into a million pieces. I was engulfed by a monster who resented Gisel for who she was, but loved the control on her feeble mind. I wept day and night for the people I mistakenly thought loved me. For all I know now is that they loved me at my best but couldn't handle me at my worst, when I needed them most. Insignificant relationships need to be erased from your life immediately if you wish to progress and thrive.

This is where this common analogy 'words are meaningless unless actions speak otherwise' comes into play. Telling someone you love them and showing someone you genuinely love them are two different things. Despite being miles apart, being there for someone whilst not knowing how to help is another. So, next time you invest in any relationship, whether it is in hospital or the outside world, ask yourself if it's going to enhance your life or wellbeing.

Remember, some people will remain as passers-by at the pit stops in one's life, but some will leave an imprint that cannot be erased, destroyed or replaced.

CHAPTER 3

The struggle

What is a tick box diagnosis?

There is no perfect diagnosis and treatment method that satisfies everyone, whether the patient or the clinicians themselves, especially when it comes down to something as unpredictable as our mental health. Funnily enough, we may have witnessed the greatest technological advances of all time and uncovered scientific revelations that have led to transforming our world for the better, but we are still yet to find an effective cure for this deadly disease that is swallowing our community as a whole.

This is down to the fact that everyone's needs are different, even though some appear to fall under the same umbrella because of the similarities between the experiences or symptoms felt. We are all individuals at the end of the day. Although our DNA may be 99.9 per cent genetically identical, there are undeniable differences between each one of us. Just look around you. That 0.1 per cent does not only come down to our exterior, but also the foundations that make up our personality, interests and core beliefs. There are factors that are dependent on the environment such as upbringing, facilities provided, effective treatment and how early on it is implemented. Although, in principle, it is true that we dictate our future, but this is only to a certain extent, as there are aspects of our lives that we have very little control over. This is in respect to the treatment that patients can access depending on where their home is situated, their financial stability, cultural background and even the consequential effect the illness has on their loved ones, which can potentially influence their response and support during this difficult period.

Treatment for an ED is a partnership where a give-and-take relationship is the only way to optimise the chances of full recovery, because clinicians will not have a magic wand to put an end to your sorrows as much as they wish to, nor will you be able to fight this alone and be triumphant. Clinicians need to take an active role in their patient's recovery, in order to boost the sufferer's chances of reclaiming their life back, which can save the NHS millions and, most importantly, save many lives in the process. Two birds with one stone!

Sometimes, as patients and human beings, we are all so wrapped up in our problems that we fail to realise clinicians are people too, who may or may not have had a similar experience to us. In fact, they probably have a past that they wish to forget about, too. Their present won't just involve blue lights and cardiac arrests. They likely also feel apprehensive about what is next.

It is as frustrating for the consultant and the team involved, as it is for a loved one or the patient themselves when things don't go to plan. Don't be alarmed if more bumps appear on the road than first anticipated – this is completely normal. If everything was plain-sailing, then recovery isn't worth it. Why bother even attempting it in the first place, when the option of remaining ill seems as good or even better? Think about it; I wouldn't be investing my time into writing this book, if I didn't strongly believe this was a problem worth addressing and I thought I had even the slightest chance of transforming someone's life.

It is abnormal to be normal

Frustratingly, the anorexic label may not leave you for some time, even after overcoming potentially the biggest bump in your journey. You now find yourself in an ideal position, whereby you are able to close this chapter of your life once and for all and start afresh. You are happy as can be and you see things that you couldn't see before because you are no longer blinded by anorexia and her toxic ways. She no longer encapsulates every thought in your head and determines every action that takes place. You are finally (somewhat) in control. This is not a pit that you can't find your way out of nor a story without a climax, now you know it for yourself.

If I were to describe anorexia to my 11-year-old self, I would struggle to find the words because it is an illness that doesn't quite make sense. To this day, I can't get my head around it, despite consecutive relapses and numerous admissions into different inpatient settings. There is no such thing as a "know-it-all" anorexic, because presentations may be similar and the diagnosis may fall under the same umbrella, but no two people are the same. Manifestations vary from person to person depending on age, experiences, personality traits and other environmental factors, so clinicians are reluctant to use a generic plan for all sufferers as a way of achieving a full recovery. When treating both a personality disorder and an eating disorder, it is much like a chicken and egg situation, on who came first and whether that really matters in the first place. Your personality disorder may well encompass the traits of an eating disorder: destructive behaviours and manifestations that make your illness unique and different from someone else with the same diagnosis.

When you are in the depths of anorexia, every command dictated by it is for the better in your eyes. Letting go of this "favourable" friend becomes a bizarre concept and compliance during treatment goes out of the window. This demeaning and resentful voice, this monster possessing your mind and body, becomes your everything. Hiding food, pacing relentlessly, purging your guts out, trapped in a vicious cycle of restriction, taking laxatives as though it's a sweet became the norm. This is the hidden life of a struggling anorexic on an eating disorder ward and within the community. This does not incorporate everyone and, to make it clear, nor am I suggesting that every unit is like this. These are the behaviours that are commonly found in institutions similar to where I was; they are what I experienced first-hand and what I witnessed on a daily basis.

In EDUs, it is very common to find yourself trapped in these behaviours for a prolonged period of time, as well as adopting new ones. These adoptions are a similar concept to picking up behaviours from peers, due to the sheer amount of time you spend with them. It is our nature as humans intertwined with our separate personality traits. External factors affect our response leading up to things and, consequently, our actions afterwards are highly influenced by the setting we are placed in and the people we are surrounded by. It is unusual to not have these behaviours in an EDU and becomes abnormal to be normal. Fitting into the criteria for a diagnosis of anorexia is the norm. If you display behaviours that outdo anorexia and her demands, it is seen as disobedience and not being "sick enough" to need treatment, which shouldn't be the case. We should all be pursuing a life beyond this, however hard it may be to comprehend in the harder moments. My advice is to not let the behaviours of others get the better of you. The fight should be between you and anorexia only, not anyone else. Everyone else is going through their own journey and those helping you are there to serve their duty of care.

Is it normal to be abnormal?

This question can be answered or interpreted in various ways, but what I would suggest is that in a dysfunctional restricted environment such as an EDU, we encounter various problems, most of which are very much interlinked with the nature or severity of the eating disorder, but others can be adopted due to the culture and morale of the ward at the time. The ward environment should not be undermined or dismissed as not playing a part in patients' progress, because it does so regardless of whether it is seen in a positive or negative light. An example of this is during my stay in multiple psychiatric hospitals, all of which impacted my life one way or another. First and foremost, the NHS did save a broken 15-year-old girl who was in the midst of despair and thought it was the end. Then, all of a sudden, she was relieved of some of the pain she was forced to endure for so long and was able to regain the ability to pick up a knife and fork without her inner voice always looming over her and taking advantage of her feeble mind. She sometimes had the courage to even say "No" to the illness controlling every limb of her body from top to bottom, and that showed that an inpatient setting can live up to the expectations it promises.

The list doesn't end there: the safe platform it provides helps in the learning of new skills and applying these transferable skills to the next step of recovery, however that may look for you as an individual aligned by your future goals. The other additional bonus is being able to piece together that missing element of trust in everyone and everything, by forming healthy relationships between the staff and the patients. Last but not least, it helps to build up resilience and strength in order to feel triumphant over any obstacle, no matter how big or small. The girl featured in this chapter was myself, but many may be able to relate to this regardless of whether you are a girl or not.

I truly believe that there is no harder, more strenuous and tiresome battle than fighting ourselves or what appears to be us, when, in fact, it is a parasite festering in our minds that won't let go. We can fail to recognise this and remain in denial, but the majority of the time it has such a strong grip that cannot be broken by the use of a knife or a weapon, and it needs a hospital to slowly but surely help tear one away from the struggles that have now become one's identity.

On the contrary, I also found myself adopting unhelpful and even life-threatening behaviours that I didn't walk through the hospital doors with. It is somewhat similar to a child's early developmental years being influenced by their surroundings and why teenagers and adults fall into peer or social pressures. This is not to discourage anyone from accepting treatment from an inpatient unit, but to ensure that they know what they are signing up to and to advise that they be wary of their surroundings and the people they associate with. Without a shadow of a doubt, there will be ups and downs, but as long as the trajectory overall is in the upwards direction, this is a huge achievement. I cannot stress enough the importance of focusing on your own recovery, however hard it may be. Sharing other people's burdens while you are in a vulnerable position will exacerbate your problems, which won't do either of you any good. A very wise staff member – who I will keep anonymous, but for the time being call "Robin" – once told me that we wouldn't normally loan money out if we were in the depths of debt, unless we were planning to become bankrupt. This would be foolish and the only situation you would be able to do so is when you have surplus, so that you are not compromising your financial stability.

I don't think having a mental illness makes me special, but rather human. I am just a normal human being burdened by unrealistic expectations imposed by society and insecurities that arise due to this. It is fair to say that we, as a generation, are very much stuck in the pursuit of acceptance and conforming to the norm, or what is believed to be the norm by society at the time, to the point that we lose sight of our attributes and achievements on an individual basis.

What are compensatory behaviours?

To all GPs, doctors, nurses, medics or anyone in the medical field, open your eyes and look around you. The harsh reality is that the world is slowly but surely being consumed by an illness that many are still oblivious to. A whole generation could be easily wiped away in front of your very own eyes.

One simple way to prevent or, at least, prolong this from occurring is by being able to identify key compensatory behaviours in the early stages, even before delving deep into the hows and whys.

Compensatory behaviours can vary from sufferer to sufferer, even if two people fall under the same umbrella term 'Anorexia Nervosa'. This illness is so complex that we are yet to find a cure that works for everyone. Each case presents with numerous struggles but of the same nature; others have co-morbid diagnoses, requiring even more specialist treatment and so forth. This is why treatment has to be tailored to the individual according to their immediate needs at the time and is also one of the underlying reasons why sufferers take, on average, a hefty six years to make a full recovery – which is already 30 per cent of my lifetime so far. There are different presentations and struggles, as well as unexpected bumps or lapses, along the way, which won't be the same for everyone.

"Eating disorder" is a very generalised term used to indicate various mental health conditions, all of which can potentially have a detrimental impact on the sufferer's wellbeing, both mentally and physically. For instance, the distinguishing factor is the BMI range you are classed in, which reinforces the misconception that in order for you to be diagnosed with anorexia, you have to be nothing but skin and bones. This is not at all an indication of a person's mental state, especially in the beginning stages where sufferers are told they are not "sick enough" for treatment. This, in turn, gives the illness more time to manifest lasting effects that could have been avoidable in the first place if there wasn't such a lack of understanding. What happened to the idea that prevention is the best cure? Below are some examples of compensatory behaviours.

Abusing laxatives

The best way to describe laxatives from a recovering anorexic's point of view is that it is the biggest marketing scam for ineffective "weight loss". If you can avoid going down this path completely, I strongly advise you to do so and if it has ever crossed your mind, then I hope I can make you realise it is not worth the time and pain. For others who are stuck in this vicious cycle of addiction, I hope I can make even the slightest difference and deter you from using any more or give you the voice to talk about your struggles openly without the element of shame attached to it. Laxatives can usually be picked up from any supermarket shelf and are primarily used for relieving short-term constipation – note "short-term". However, using it in excess, like any other medication, can have detrimental side effects. For laxatives, these include an increased risk of irreversible damage to your bowels, which might not always be visible to the human eye, but hinders you from being able to pass stools normally and prolongs the time for peristalsis to occur. It can also lead to severe constipation that is hard to resolve without weaning off laxatives completely and allowing your bowels time to regain the ability to function on their own, as it was always meant to do in the first place. Unfortunately, this may take days, weeks, months and even years for some, depending on the impact it had on their bodily functions, whether the disruptions caused are reversible and how long they have been reliant on laxatives. During the early reduction stages, the pros of abusing laxatives may well appear to outshine the cons, but nothing will eradicate even a fraction of the uncomfortable, painful trauma you will most likely end up experiencing. The pain will be intolerable at times, your bloat may well look as though you are nine months' pregnant and seeing the number on the scale jump by kilos each day will scare the living daylights out of an anorexia sufferer. Should you carry on abusing laxatives, I can assure you it will only get harder to manage. You are inflicting additional unnecessary pain on yourself in replacement for what? Some water loss?

It is known to be a susceptible period of time, where you need to be closely monitored regarding not only the use of laxatives, but the toll it is taking on your body. This is extremely important as a sufferer is more inclined to resort back to them for temporary relief when they see their worst nightmare (weight gain) become a reality.

Some of the other side effects of an excessive dependence on laxatives is that you have to go to the toilet constantly, you're unsure as to when you'll soil yourself again, and you sit on the toilet for hours with bits of food mixed with water and blood ejecting from both ends (diarrhoea and vomiting). You have that satisfying feeling of emptiness, until the dreaded next meal, where you find yourself ballooning after a bowl of cereal. It makes you question whether cutting down what you eat is the best solution or whether taking another senna tablet is. This vicious cycle will only get harder to break; the longer you leave it to thrive, the more fatal the repercussions become and they can lead to irreversible damage to your bowels and digestive tract, making you more susceptible to infections such as C.Difficle. It is not unusual to find those suffering with this addiction have a shorter life expectancy. It begins with just one senna tablet – it's a medication after all. However, just like anything else in life, if not used appropriately it can cause more harm than good. So, next time you pay £4.99 for another "harmless" packet of senna tablets to resolve your short-term constipation, don't just think about how it is draining your wallet, but whether there is an actual need for it and whether it is worth the tremendous pain that follows?

Purging

This is a compensatory behaviour that I am not familiar with personally, but I have seen many of my friends in hospital struggle with this and how it impedes every bit of their lives. Eating food is a battle in itself when suffering from an eating disorder, but then you find yourself left to endure this overriding feeling of guilt afterwards. It is not all about the food in ED recovery, it is important to monitor the behaviours pre and post meal and come up with a way for each individual to cope with the difficult feelings triggered. Otherwise the psychological fight only gets harder to contend with and it is not an effective method of treatment. In order for an admission to serve its purpose successfully first time around, the core of the problem needs to be treated, not only by touching the surface but also the behaviours that coincide with it. Latching onto these behaviours can be a desperate measure for someone suffering from an ED – as absurd as it may sound, it is the only means by which they can prolong the inevitable weight gain process and have some control.

Instead what needs to happen is for that control to be taken away completely by those who are caring for the patient, so that any remaining temptation is eradicated, because this illness is deceptive. If it means locking the toilets after every meal for at least an hour or full toilet supervision and close monitoring, then, as extreme as it sounds, so be it. It is not unusual for the urge to become even more unbearable at times when the anorexia feels as though it is being challenged and sufferers may resort to discrete opportunistic behaviours, like the misuse of plastic bags or bins for the purpose of purging. It is far from pleasant seeing a friend throw up their dinner in the middle of the main corridor because of utter desperation. She had no access to anywhere she could do it at the time and all I could do was watch helplessly. Society needs to open its eyes to the brutal fact that it only takes one instance of purging to induce a heart attack. I am not going to sugar-coat this matter because I've seen it take many precious lives and I can't bear to see anyone else fall victim to it. The consequences of purging religiously include disintegrating your teeth enamel and greater vulnerability to major weight fluctuations, which only heightens emotions and induces the urge to binge or restrict further. Doctors are most concerned about the electrolyte imbalance, severe dehydration and, eventually, every organ in your body failing, leaving you at the brink of death. I cannot think of one effective benefit of purging. It is not something that we use or do in society, like exercise or the temporary use of laxatives for medicinal purposes. It is best to stop cold turkey if you can or, at least, progressively decrease the number of times you do it until it is no longer a problem. However scary the weight gain may seem, I can assure you the weight gain does slow down. Understandably, it will take time and you will have to endure some pain and discomfort, but not half as much as if you had continued engaging in the behaviour in the long run. It affects you and those who care about you and value your presence. It is similar to a piece of land that has undergone drought for several months, hoping for just a drop of rain to moisten the soil and give the flowers even an opportunity to rejuvenate. Then, all of a sudden, there is this torrential rain. The natural reaction for the soil that's been deprived of water for so long is to suck in every bit of water it can. Soon, the empty riverbanks start to fill up to normal levels, in fear of another drought. In anorexia recovery, this refers to not gaining weight for the sake of it or because a doctor has advised you to do so, but regaining weight that should have never been lost in the first place.

Overexercising

This topic is very relevant to me. We hear in the news that the minimal physical activity expected of us in a day as healthy adults is 10,000 steps, as it's proven to optimise our health and wellbeing and prevent other complications from arising – obesity, type 2 diabetes induced by an unhealthy lifestyle (combination of exercise regime and diet), etc. "Overexercising" goes against every rule or idea society has imposed upon us in this day and age. Unfortunately, some are oblivious to its existence, because exercise is promoted as being crucial to a healthy lifestyle and nobody openly talks about the repercussions faced with excessive exercise, which can be just as detrimental or even cost you your life. As they say, everything in life is good in moderation. So, next time you are eager for your child to join all the extracurricular activities, such as football, netball and karate, just be aware of whether it is becoming an unhelpful obsession for them, rather than something that they find pleasure from. It should never be forced by loved ones in the hope that it creates opportunities. It is always better that the interest comes from them and they are willing to commit to it for the right reasons, not through peer pressure as a way of changing themselves to fit into the crowd or to address underlying insecurities about their body. It might start with losing a little bit of weight or, what we refer to as, becoming "fitter". It can spiral so easily from one kilogram to some more, and then you are left seeing your child deteriorate to the point that they no longer resemble a healthy 14-year-old but a walking skeleton. It is as though they have been stripped of everything: their laugh, their sarcastic comments, their quirky sense of humour, their good school grades, the role of the best advice-giver any friend could ask for and that annoying little sister, who finds pleasure in irritating her older brother. This illness is toxic and it's a reality that many parents are facing.

We, as humans, can never get food consumption spot on. There are periods in life where we find comfort in indulging in food and other times where anything from a mouthful of food to a sip of water becomes impossible to swallow. This can be a natural response and indicates how we are feeling or whether there are mitigating circumstances. For instance, during mourning, it is very common that many restrict their intake, sometimes not even intentionally, but as a maladaptive coping mechanism to deal with the ordeal. In some cultures, it is a way of showing respect to those who have just passed away, especially if they are a part of your immediate family. In Anorexia Nervosa, restriction can begin with swapping certain food types that you used to enjoy, to the "healthier" lower calorie options. A Muller corner can turn into a pot of Muller Light, or a Philadelphia tub can change into a lighter version. Such behaviours usually go unnoticed and anorexia may start to slowly creep in. "Calories" is mistakenly seen as a forbidden term that means becoming fatter, when, in actual fact, it is just a unit of measure of the energy that your body requires to survive. So, then, why do you find yourself setting this maximum calorie intake goal, which decreases as each day progresses to sustain the level of weight loss? The miniscule amount you are consuming isn't enough for a person in the depths of a coma who cannot move a limb or mutter a word, so why are you torturing yourself to lose a couple of pounds? You don't need to nor can you afford to. However, all too quickly, you will be half the body weight you were and will find everyday tasks as simple as walking to school or doing a local shopping run too tiresome to do – even the thought induces that nervous flutter in the back of your stomach, but then not engaging makes you feel even more guilty. There is no resolution to this problem that will satisfy both your illness and your starving body. The flurry of compliments come all at once, one after the other at the start. This reinforces the false belief that losing weight is equivalent to looking better and soon it has gone "too far". It is no longer regarded as attractive, but believe me when I say that no anorexic – including myself – is under any illusion that looking thin, so that the rib cage is on show, collar bones protrude and thigh gaps are on display, means that we are any more attractive than those of a healthy weight. In all honesty, it is the opposite; with every pound we lose, self-confidence disintegrates to the point that it is no longer existent. This illness doesn't stem from vanity as much as it may appear to do so, especially to those of you who haven't ever experienced or come across it before. Think of it as a parasite that has invaded your body without your permission, drained all of your resources in order for it to keep thriving, grown uncontrollably to the point that it is difficult to remove and all that you are left facing is the unfair consequences of it all, and the mental and physical effect it has on you and your body. No matter how significant the weight loss is, your anorexia remains unsatisfied and all you witness in the mirror in utter disgust is this fat blubbering mess. Hence why we are so wrapped up in the lies anorexia feeds us. Hiding food is also a deceptive behaviour that sufferers tend to adopt. If you are anything like my gullible parents, the phrase, "I've already had lunch" is good enough, because they trust their child infinitely and cannot imagine them saying even a white lie, let alone become a compulsive liar. However, there will always come a time where every lie is brought to the surface, especially in the instance where your mum finds £100 in your uniform pocket just as she is about to put the clothes in the wash. As much as she hates to acknowledge it, she knows very well it is an accumulation of £5 notes they gave me each day in hopes that I would buy lunch for myself at school. There is no other feeling comparable to the overriding guilt when you know you have let someone down. However, it is even more painful in this instance, because those people were not just somebody to you, they were your everybody. This situation is specific to me and refers to me and my family, and it may not apply to all. My parents never failed to remind me how much I was loved and valued. They celebrated every triumph and held my hand in times of hardship, every step of the way.

Sometimes we forget the impact this illness has on those around us; we are too preoccupied by our struggles that we fail to recognise it is painful for them to watch, too – more than we can imagine. Not having the experience to help adequately makes them feel powerless and deludes them with the false belief that they are incapable parents, which is far from the case. So, next time you begin to engage in another compensatory behaviour, think about the impact it would have on those around you. I know it's easier said than done, but doing so pushes you onwards on the path to recovery.

Body checking and body dysmorphia

These two topics are very much intertwined and they are not compensatory behaviours as such. However, they can be an early indication of the presence of a (potential) problem, even if it is not to the extent of Anorexia Nervosa. Body dysmorphia is a topic that is often trivialized and described as seeing a "fatter" version of yourself in a mirror. Instead, it needs to be recognised as a mental disorder that encourages a distorted perception of the body. This means that you may be overly focused on faults and imperfections, when these are actually just a part of what makes you an individual. We may not always be satisfied with the reflection in the mirror. As humans, we have a habit of scrutinising ourselves and picking out things to change, whether it is our body shape, our composition or stature, the colour of our skin, having facial features such as dimples or freckles. We are also tied down by things that are beyond our control, i.e. height, foot size and the colour of our skin. I believe all imperfections are perfections and a person's importance shouldn't be based on a thigh gap or voluptuous curvy body. It should be based on the respect and kindness you show to others, the honesty in every word you say and allowing yourself to make mistakes, so that you can learn from them. There is no such thing as perfection and that's okay. I am more inclined to be friends with someone who stays true to who they are and does not let the world change their smile. Unfortunately, as much as I dream for this ideal world to become a reality, our society breeds pretentious people and so the need to attain what is considered as an ideal body is on the forefront of everyone's mind at one point or another.

For instance, I don't think there has been a single occasion where I haven't heard a lady complaining about her cellulite. Cellulite is far from abnormal; it is fat deposited on areas such as the buttocks and thighs, and appears similar to how dimples look. It tends to happen to women rather than men because women **have** and **need** a higher percentage of fat in their bodies. This shouldn't be seen as a misfortune. It is your biological make-up and it allows life processes such as fertilisation to occur.

It is your mind that tells you that you can't wear a pair of shorts or a bikini on a hot day. It is your mindset alone and judgements are inevitable. The way you manage to handle judgement is what shows true maturity and sets a good example for the next generation to follow, so that they are not too preoccupied by this endless pursuit for a "perfect" body. After all, you already have one that is perfect for you. There is no greater gift than having the ability to breathe in the fresh air, walk with ease, talk freely, hear the cockerels crow in the morning – definitely not in London, though, where sensory experiences would more likely include hearing the hecticness of a bustling city, tasting amazing foods from across the world, smelling the blooming flowers as winter fades and spring starts to come alive. It is about taking the opportunity to embrace whatever life gives you. That should be our focus and we should not take it for granted.

Even though I've only mentioned body dysmorphia in women so far, it is something that can target men, too. This could arise due to multiple reasons, one of which is insecurity about their body. Many youngsters today are driven by other people's opinions and by what is portrayed in the media (bad and good), especially if it optimises the chances of masculinity and thereby the chance of impressing a girl or looking "cool" (I am cringing as I write these words). I am not a boy, but I can assure you that you have the rest of your life ahead of you to find the "one", whoever that may be. Enjoy the time you have being young and the mischievousness that goes with it. Do not get tied down by commitments you are not capable of managing at the moment. Since you are still trying to figure out who you are and what your identity is, try and feel relaxed about relationships and the stresses of school.

Do you think all these six-pack henchmen have had an easy life, with their main aim being to have a swarm of girls chasing after them? No is the (most likely) answer, because nobody knows what happens behind closed doors. These very same people could have been victims of severe bullying; they might have been teased about their weight or body composition, and lived in fear that the world detested them for it. All they are doing is what they know best, which is to respond to the world and adhere to its expectations.

Unfortunately, the world has tampered with the idea of love and attraction, relating it too much to the way we look. It's not uncommon for many to spend hours at the gym to shed that extra pound or to spend entire savings on "metabolism booster" tablets – one of the biggest marketing scams I have come across. Also, you might be aware of the wide range of protein shakes available. In my opinion, they taste absolutely putrid and similar to, what I call, powdered water with odd flavours. Remember, too, that love doesn't have to mean a happy romantic relationship. It could also be seeking acceptance or fitting in with a friendship group or a community group.

Body-checking is a behaviour that often goes unnoticed, because if you don't suffer from it, it is not easy to identify. I've found myself spending hours on end in front of a mirror, posing in different positions until seeing something that was "satisfactory" enough for my anorexia to leave me in peace.

This meant that in every shopping centre I visited, rather than edging towards the clothes sections as you normally do, I was desperately hunting for the nearest mirror, even if it meant I was going in and out of every shop on the site empty-handed, avoiding eye contact with the security to alleviate the embarrassment. At home, if something didn't look quite right or I found it too exposing, you would find it lurking in the back of the wardrobe, never to be touched again – regardless of how much it cost. I may take a thousand selfies, but there won't be one that I like, because all I can see is this massive, unlovable, repulsive body, which doesn't deserve to be exposed to the rest of the world. This has meant that I've been reluctant about attending social gatherings or anything that involves other people. During my teenage years, this posed a hurdle, especially when trying to rekindle friendships or make new ones. My low self-esteem and low self-confidence weren't resolved with body-checking. In fact, it was a factor that played a major role in sustaining that feeling. I have spent sleepless nights with tears streaming down my face because I was no longer able to wrap both of my hands around my thigh. I felt unbearable disgust at my thighs touching and at the realisation that all of the hard work I'd put into achieving a thigh gap had been such a waste.

These symptoms are commonly misunderstood and are incorrectly linked to vanity, when, in actual fact, it is the opposite. They arise from insecurities. My insecurities made me measure every inch of my body, from the top of my head to the bottom of my ankles; I was unable to pick an outfit or find the will to wake up each morning because of all the racing derogatory thoughts in my head. Starving my already feeble body and putting myself through torture to achieve something that was unattainable in the first place wasn't one of my wisest choices. But this illness is so manipulative that it can use your strengths against you and fool even the brightest people into believing delusions and erratic thoughts. I, for one, took every word that anorexia said on board.

Self-harm

This is a term that often gets misinterpreted or dismissed as an "attention-seeking" behaviour, when in actual fact it is a maladaptive coping strategy that someone has adopted to control their overwhelming emotions and an ineffective way of feeling in tune with emotions by inflicting pain upon oneself. It often occurs when someone is going through a period of change, facing abuse of any sort or dealing with unfortunate events. There are numerous reasons why someone resorts to self-harming. It needs to be acknowledged that self-harming doesn't always mean cutting arms nor does it always entail friction burns, which provides the longed-for stinging sensation. Having notable scars all across your body is not a way of flaunting or seeking attention. This topic shouldn't be taken so lightly; people who self-harm are more inclined to distance themselves from others, hide their scars in embarrassment and live the remainder of their lives in silent suffering. Until what point, though? When waking up in the morning becomes unbearable to comprehend? When you feel ostracized by the world and find yourself at the cusp of suicide? This is when it is considered "important enough" to be addressed and intervention is initiated. Even so, this does not mean you will automatically have a therapist and a psychiatrist assigned to you to optimise your chances of a full recovery as quickly as possible. Instead, prepare yourself to be another name added onto an endless waiting list of people, scattered all across the country, in utter desperation for any help at all. Remember, too, that it won't only affect them; just imagine how painful it is for loved ones to watch their closest slipping away, reclining to their room and wasting their days not being able to see tomorrow.

This is not to say we shouldn't put our trust in the NHS and the mental health services available. We should appreciate the wide range of facilities on offer, which the rest of the world is crying out for. The NHS is not perfect and there is certainly room for improvement, but that is an ongoing problem that cannot be solved overnight – perhaps not even in the upcoming months or years, as disheartening as it may sound. In the meantime, the best way to support your loved one during any period of uncertainty is to prioritise their safety above everything else. This does not necessarily mean stripping them of their freedom, but rather having an open and honest conversation about how to move forwards. Tell them how much they are loved and valued each day, that their existence isn't a waste of space, that they are an asset to the family and, above all, that they are enough just the way they are. This could potentially save a person's life – or, at least, make someone's day that little bit more tolerable.

I am not going to sit here and write about different methods of self-harm that you need to be aware of, because I know that this book is not going to be picked up by anyone walking down a shopping aisle, but someone who might be directly affected. It is not my intention to give people ideas. I am more than happy to share ideas in regard to what could help you get through a rough patch. Punishing yourself is not the solution to any problem, however much grief your head gives you or as compensation for every tear shed by your loved ones.

During periods of heightened emotions or arousal, or times where you would commonly resort to self-harm as a coping mechanism, instead immerse your face or hands in ice-cold water to relieve the intensity of your emotions. I personally found that decluttering my thoughts and vocalising my feelings to someone I truly trusted helped me to rationalise things and to think in a different perspective. The above might not be feasible for everyone, particularly if you feel as though there isn't a trustworthy figure in your life.

The internet has earned a bad reputation in terms of the psychological and emotional impact it can have on young people, but if used appropriately, it can be a great tool in aiding someone with a mental disorder. There are registered websites created with this purpose in mind, so that you don't have to fight the battle alone. Even if you are unable to access the internet, there are phone helplines that are more than willing to respond, such as Samaritans, MIND, Rethink, Beat and more.

There are, at least, 450 million people in the entire world, as well as numerous others who are yet to be diagnosed or go unnoticed. For the rest of us, we cannot deny the fact that we, too, struggle with fluctuating mental health states (including mood) at different points in our lives. If not, how can you distinguish between the good and bad days, and why do different situations evoke different emotional responses?

The three simple tips below might help you to get through the times of anxiety that swoop in suddenly, so that you can prevent them from ballooning into a panic attack or an escalation.

1. Essential oils, such as lemon and eucalyptus, are found to be good for grounding; lavender can help to relieve stress, and peppermint is found to boost energy levels and aid digestion. Studies have been conducted on the impact of essential oils for relieving stress and anxiety from those suffering, which is a very common occurrence, and aromatherapy has positive results. For me, as an inpatient in my fourth inpatient unit, having a "warmie" was the norm. Personally, it was more of a comfort thing; my "warmie" had a lot of sentimental value to it, as it was a present for my 20th from my brother, who lived 130 miles away, but through my "warmie" was right by my side. To clarify, a "warmie" is a cuddly toy version of a hot water bottle. It is something tangible and can help with grounding oneself in the present moment. Essential oils can be

also put on it, so it holds many purposes both in an inpatient unit and at home, where, in fact, such things should come into practice as much as possible as a means of self-soothing.

2. Other mini gadgets that are widely available are fidget cubes, tangles, stress balls and so on. These are only a handful of handy gadgets that won't cost you a fortune and, most importantly, could prevent you from waiting at A&E for hours one night at crisis point.

3. Distraction is a helpful tool to calm certain situations and to take control of your emotions, especially during the important stage where self-harming behaviours are more likely to happen. Some ideas that have worked for me were drawing and writing how I was feeling at the time as a way of expression, engaging in some form of exercise (for the right reasons, of course) – preferably a walk with someone, listening to nostalgic or uplifting music, watching a favourite TV series or a good movie, and self-soothing techniques, such as attending to personal care, having a hot shower, pampering yourself, etc. These suggestions won't work for everyone and won't be the magic cure. They act as a temporary relief so that emotions don't get the better of you (at least) this time around.

For some, exerting any built-up energy is important, in order to prevent the situation from spiralling out of control. The aim is to overcome the adrenaline rush in any way possible, so use the time wisely. Some of my suggestions would be hitting a pillow, having a cry, bawling your eyes out, screaming from the top of your lungs, and tensing and relaxing your muscles. Destructive behaviours should not be on the cards and they do not show progression. Do everything in your power, regardless of whether you are the sufferer or a loved one, to avoid this situation ballooning and reoccurring. That's not to say you will never feel like this again, because you may do and I would be lying if I said otherwise. The only difference next time around is that you will know how to deal with it accordingly, as you're equipped with the skills and support to do so.

In any moment where you are in a great state of arousal or distress – which may or may not be due to an obvious trigger at the time, but a build-up of emotions – you are more likely to engage in behaviours that supposedly help release energy in an attempt to diminish any last remaining bit of pain brewing inside. This is because you've got nothing else to offer, no transferable skills (as yet) nor self-soothing techniques, and you are left facing the potentially irreversible repercussions of this deadly illness. If there is a way in, there is a way out, even if it is the same way you came in. So, give some of these suggestions a go, but be warned that not every one will be your cup of tea.

Why having somebody is better than having nobody

This illness can be very isolating, regardless of whether you undergo hospitalisation or not. It carries many misconceptions and stigma, which makes people more reluctant to share struggles in case they aren't considered "important enough". Perhaps you are always living in the fear of burdening someone else and this means there is a higher likelihood of abandonment, which exacerbates the problem and is a feeling many diagnosed with BPD (and perhaps co-morbid disordered eating) share.

I am lucky enough to say that I have a family who has shown me what unconditional love means. In my eyes, once you've experienced it, there is nothing else that can compare to it. Each one of them has been there for me, despite me constantly pushing them away to the point that anyone else would have instantly backed away. They stood back at times, if need be, and they knew when to get a bit more involved, without me having to vocalise my struggles or needs. Our family has only got stronger as each day passes, because of the ups and downs. This resulted in the bond being tampered with from time to time, but it was never completely pulled apart.

My parents would go above and beyond to keep a smile on our faces (both me and my older brother), and they worked incredibly hard to the point that they were exhausted and aching at the end of the day. Nonetheless, they never thought twice about getting up the next morning to do it all over again. This was because they wouldn't be able to stand the thought of their little bundles of joy going to bed hungry or to feel any discomfort, even if that meant rotating between two jobs and cutting out "unnecessary" pleasures for themselves, including a comfortable mattress to sleep on. A sofa bed was more than enough for them and they found greater comfort and contentment knowing that their two children were sleeping on a bed, feeling well fed and cared for. It wasn't a 5-star hotel – nothing like it, in fact – but it was something more than any best-rated hotel could ever offer. It was my home, a place where I felt welcomed, safe and didn't have to please anyone – i.e. I could leave it in a tip (preferably not!). It may not have had the finest cuisine from all corners of the world, but it had my mum's cooking, which tasted far better because the main ingredient was nothing more than a sprinkle of love and joy, without a single moan or groan from her even once. Yes, I couldn't indulge in the comfort of a king-sized bed with memory foam so that I could have that elusive feeling of sleeping on clouds, but I was snuggled up under several layers of blankets that I could call my own with my nine-year-old brother next to me.

I had an army of people to support me along the way and for that I am eternally grateful. Many don't have such support and I should take the time to count my blessings, rather than dwelling on what was wrong.

CHAPTER 4

Life carries on...

Letters to friends

This letter is addressed directly to some very special people who have been a part of my life for the last 15 months. Their imprint cannot be erased, destroyed or replaced, and each one of them has made a poignant impact on my life for the better. Bethlem was not just a roof to stay under, nor was it a place filled with only joyous memories, but it became the home I longed for, and the community there became my most trusted family, who I would share my joys and sorrows with. They guided me through the roughest of days and held my hand every step of the way.

The list is endless, but what I admire the most about you all and what sets you apart from the rest of SLaM (South London and Maudsley NHS Foundation Trust) is your willingness and belief in every single patient that walks through the doors, no matter how much of a "handful" their history makes them out to be, no matter whether they are classed as a SEED (Severe and Enduring Eating Disorders) patient or not, and regardless of whether they are dismissed as a revolving door patient or they're completely new to the system. Everyone is welcomed with open arms and encouraged to pursue a full recovery or, at least, a life that is worth living for, because no one is dismissed as a lost cause or a waste of time.

You have all helped me see that the impossible is, in fact, possible, if you can adopt an 'I can' and 'I will' mentality over time. Regardless of my dips, however low it went, even at the verge of death, none of you ever gave into the eating disorder that consumed me nor the BPD that was constantly bullying my mind. What you did instead was to congratulate me for getting this far and encourage me to have a fresh start tomorrow.

When I was ready to admit defeat, you reminded me of how strong I am and that I wouldn't leave an exam half completed or do any job half-heartedly because of the fear of failure. So why did this principle not apply to my recovery? Don't let your fears drive away your dreams or deter you from pursuing the life you wish to have, the people you want to meet, the things you want to learn and the love for yourself you wish to regain. Capture every moment and take a shot at life; if it is blurry or not quite right the first time around, just keep trying again and again, because you have nothing more to lose and so much more to gain.

To Dearest Sid the Sloth Sarah, The Biggest Egg/Prune Head Ian, Diva Dancer Sylvia – still Rocking her Youth, The Loveable Drugged Up Niki, Smiley Best Mum Nicola, 'Are you okay?' Cheerful Ryan, Best Dressed Queen Yinka, The BO Producer Fabian (who is also a part of the furniture), Loved Up Newly Married Mr D, Angel Mumma Norma, OT (the "fun" people, hosting quizzes I can't win on purpose, of course, *cough cough*, Nike), the Brain Team (the medical & psychology team, both the good and the bad), Vegan Corellete (my mum's beautiful pronunciation), Maria's PA (Sastri), the Odd Irish Lady who I can't understand half of the time Emma, Boss Baby Biggest (softy) Lynn, 'God bless you' Helen, Pamper Queen Cagla, Hibernating Juliet, to all those who have decided to be so "inconsiderate" and get pregnant, take extended leave or the traitors that have moved on, Loudspeaker Laura, Dream Team Night Crew (Tam, whose Best Friend is also called Sarcasm, Anthony the Guy with a Sweet Tooth, the Ruling Captain of the Shift Avette), Robert the Best Advice Giver, Everton my Friend who is also my Best Therapist, Bubbly Best Hugger Zoe, "Efficient" Physical Obs doer Ester, Nizar the World's Worst Comedian, Iron Lady Wendy and, leaving the best till last, my Inspirational Brain Guru of all times, who I am lucky enough to call my Consultant, Dr Au, as well as every other Cheerleader or Well Wisher that I have accidentally missed out (I can only apologise).

This last week, in particular, has been chaotic to say the least. It was a non-stop rollercoaster of emotions, rightfully so, and there now seems to be a void in my life that will never be adequately replaced.

To me, Bethlem wasn't just a scenic 270 acres of land to roam around in, nor was it a place filled with only joyous memories. It gave me a home that I had been longing for, rather than just a roof to stay under *and I was lucky enough (99.9 per cent of the time) to be surrounded by people who were not forced to "care" for me until they stepped out of those doors.*

Recalling my time in an EDU, there was a phrase that was recited again and again by staff that I vividly remember and it is played on repeat in my head: "It is our duty of care." This was said with the best intentions, as a way in which to reassure us that there are people who genuinely care, when, in actual fact, it can be counterproductive. It can be easily misunderstood and misinterpreted as though staff have no choice but to look after us and that is the sole purpose of why they are doing it. This can, in turn, create a division within the community, which heightens the chance of instability within the ward environment and can affect absolutely anyone and everyone there. This idea is reinforced even when we refer back to the dictionary definition of 'duty', which is the legal obligation or responsibility that one needs to abide by, otherwise there may well be consequences such as negligence, which can jeopardise one's career or be retained as a black mark on their records. This is an area of improvement that the ward could make or at least initiate, so that it sets an example for the rest of society to follow.

When you are contending with several illnesses at once, you are unable to distinguish between them and, ultimately, between you and the illness! I've spoken about my eating disorder – no, let me correct myself: I have spoken about the hideous illness that doesn't deserve a name or to be known as being in my possession. As I mentioned earlier, I am not leaving these doors claiming to be a "recovered" anorexic, but I am leaving these doors one step closer to where I want to be.

Many of you have advised and assured me repeatedly that there is light at the end of the tunnel. I've always been hesitant to believe this even half-heartedly, convinced that it was actually the headlight of a fast-approaching train and you were all lying to me. The staff at Bethlem have also opened my eyes to the harsh reality that no amount of schooling or years in university will necessarily equate to success in every aspect of life.

Although the job description may highlight the importance of experience as the number one quality needed to thrive in this field, what will set you apart from the rest is a heart filled with compassion, the willingness to learn and understand, and the ability to recognise areas for improvement.

These qualities may not be in any job description and they might not mean a qualification on your CV, but they can take you far in life. Everyone knows how to make false promises and pledges for temporary relief when a patient is in utter distress and bawling their eyes out in front of you. However, being able to admit when something is not possible or that a mistake has happened plays a crucial role in building a sense of trust between staff and patients. This was one of the many endearing qualities that Bethlem staff had, which meant it felt more like a community than Staff Vs Patients.

I have not a shadow of doubt that in a couple of years, the world will see you (Nicola) for the person you were always destined to be, a respected RMN (Registered Mental Health Nurse) and a great addition to the NHS nursing team. You are already an asset to TW2, going above and beyond to ensure the wellbeing of your patients. You know there's no better feeling than seeing the smiles on loved ones' faces when they notice the illness slowly losing its grip and, with it, the unravelling of their real son or daughter.

As well as this, Bethlem taught me some valuable life lessons that I will treasure and take on board for wherever life leads me onto next. I am hoping that with a bit of care, nourishment and exposure to high winds, this bud will soon flourish into a flower that is able to stand tall and withstand anything. The bud is no one but myself. You have loved, nurtured and watered me, especially at times where I needed an extra bit of nourishment, in hopes that I would continue to grow and blossom into the person I have always aspired to be. Now, I am walking out of these doors not claiming to be a "recovered" anorexic, but walking out of these doors one step closer to where I want to be. The credit has to go out to you all, staff and patients likewise.

Giving up was not in your dictionary, Dr K, and you never doubted or questioned my ability to get better, even when things were so bleak that the easiest thing to do would have been to let go. You've proven to me that there are capable, caring professionals within this field and you aspire to be one of them. Please keep doing what you are doing and never let the ED win you over, because you continue to transform lives, just like you did for me. The major part you played in my recovery will never go unnoticed and I am eternally grateful to you for believing in this broken 19-year-old girl, bound by her history and her overwhelming fear that the world despised her and the world would be better without her presence.

Thank you...
P.s. I hope we will cross paths again out in the real world and not in these unfortunate circumstances.

Dear EJ,

My darling, what a journey it has been so far. Without a shadow of a doubt, there were moments of uncertainty, lows and hitting rock bottom, to the extent of not being able to envision a life beyond this turmoil. However, you persevered, showed great strength and resilience when confronted with an obstacle, no matter how big or small, and used your infectious smile and words of wisdom to boost the morale of the whole patient group, in some of the darkest of times. This shows how much of a caring nature you have. The compassion you more than willingly express to those around you should, in fact, be implemented upon yourself. That is my only wish for you, even if it's a miniscule fraction to begin with – just like the card says, "All big things start small."

Your brain – no, the parasite that has infested your brain – will trick you into believing otherwise, but I want you to know you truly and utterly deserve it. Learning to accept your beautiful body with all its imperfections and differences comes with time, but learning to love your body is a far trickier process and may take years and years. Remember that your body is there not to be tortured or treated as someone else's possession. Rather, it is there to undergo life processes that keep you alive and breathing. It also gives you the strength (both mentally and physically) to combat any situation that may faze you and, on top of this, it gives you the ability to try again and again until you are triumphant. Throughout anorexia recovery, you have managed to uncover bits of your true identity by detaching yourself from ED and your body has trusted you enough for it not to be unrequited love anymore. Please use this to your advantage and not the eating disorders'.

It has been my absolute pleasure watching you grow out of the shell of a person you were when you first arrived. To know that you are finally branching out of the nest to the real world and learning how to carry the weight of your wings (which acts as the burden of your mind) and take flight by using everything you have learnt so far is incredible. It makes me feel like a proud mum, so I can only imagine what Mrs H is feeling right now about regaining her little girl once and for all. The thought of moving on, learning how to fly again and nestling on unfamiliar grounds will be frightening, but we all are only a corridor apart and make sure to utilise the amazing support you have at home when necessary. Also, seek step up as the perfect opportunity to test things out in the real world. Do not be disheartened if you fall once, twice or even three times, just please remember to dust yourself off and get back up again. The future is bright and is in arm's reach; now you can enjoy the bliss of the seaside and the home comforts of Devon. Most importantly, you are one step closer to day care, which means one step closer to breaking free completely and rebuilding a life of your own.

Sending lots of love to Mama and Papa H and, of course, to you, my beautiful EJ!!!

Best wishes,
Gisel xxx

To my dearest Hay,

I have been putting this off for a while now, not because I have nothing to say but because I have so much to say and I don't have the words to express it, nor am I able to condense it into a couple of sentences on a piece of paper.

Without a shadow of a doubt, you have had one hell of a journey, containing an unfair share of bumps and moments of uncertainty. I know these past couple of months haven't been the easiest – in fact, it has been so bloody hard, unjustifiably hard – but that is in no respect your fault. Not only have you picked yourself up after every fall, wiped every tear off your face and dusted yourself off, you have always surprised the doubters and showed us that giving up isn't a viable option even in the midst of darkness.

My only wish for you now is to persevere; utilise that inner strength and determination within you to your advantage and not the eating disorders' advantage.

Remember that the crippling voice inside your head doesn't love and care for Hayley, the young lady who has ambition, the drive to reach great heights and one of the biggest hearts I've ever known. As much as anorexia says it is your friend, who wants nothing but the best for you, it is actually your worst enemy, cunningly disguised. I will say it again and again if it makes it more believable: it is lying to you, Hayley. Every word it utters is complete bullshit (pardon my language).

Every time you stand in front of a mirror, what you witness is not a true reflection of yourself. It is actually just the aftermath, the remains of a broken soul who yearns for a life, one filled with pure agony, rather than a life containing joyous memories, the thrills of young adulthood and the desire to wake up each morning with a genuine smile − not a fake one, imprinted to mask your true emotions. I don't want you to survive for the sake of it and have to endure unbearable torture day in day out; I want you to live a contented life, brimming with opportunities and happiness, which you rightfully deserve.

Life isn't easy, nor is it fair at times. This phase may only last for a couple of minutes or hours for those who are incredibly lucky, but for some it can last for days, months or years, which feels like an eternity. Bad times may appear to be never-ending and tomorrow may not look so hopeful, maybe not even tolerable, but I know you have everything it takes to change this and become a better version of yourself in order to become a person who doesn't have to abide by anorexia's foolish, deceitful commands. Instead, it is replaced by a person who can think for themselves, sympathise with less fortunate occasions without placing blame unfairly upon oneself and learn to love the person they are, not the person they could be or could have been.

The nine-year-old Hay is still very much within you. She is trapped with shackles tightly fastened around every limb in her body, unable to move, and her mouth taped shut to stop her from crying for help. That is the domineering power of anorexia for you, an illness that is renowned for being cruel, brutal and merciless towards each of its vulnerable victims and those dear to them. Nonetheless, I want you to believe me blindly when I say that there is still a way out. It is never too late or too far into the illness that recovery becomes unattainable, including for yourself. The process itself uncovers your true identity by helping you to detach yourself from the ED, so that you are able to distinguish between the two and recognise that you are heavily reliant on the ED, even on a daily basis, and this is having a detrimental impact on your wellbeing.

Recovery is the ideal opportunity to build upon your resilience, which can be the make-or-break for a successful recovery. The WH is the best platform available for this to happen and to help you steer yourself towards the right direction or change course completely, because you are currently on the wrong path. This is only possible if you allow yourself to be receptive towards every ounce of support, helpful advice and encouragement given, as well as trust in the system and, most importantly, in yourself.

Please do not ever doubt your capability, because, frankly, you don't realise how strong you are and how far you have come, although your head may have convinced you otherwise. I can assure you that attempting a full recovery will not be anywhere near as painful as a life dictated by an ED. There is still time to dig deep to scavenge, what appears to be, the last remains of the real Hayley, because there is much more to life than being bound by an ED.

Undoubtedly, it is not uncommon for many in your position to lose the ability to envision a life beyond the four walls of a psychiatric hospital. This transition can be daunting and can induce unpredictable eruptions of overwhelming emotions – even the thought of it becomes virtually impossible to comprehend. You don't have to sacrifice the rest of your life to this manipulative illness or sabotage the great heights that you are destined to reach, which certainly go beyond the constraints placed by anorexia. It has selfishly snatched your hopes and dreams from you since you were a little girl, but it is now your turn to gain control of the steering wheel that will direct you to better prospects and the bright future you deserve.

This is turning out to be a lecture now (unintentional, of course) and I don't want to teach you how to do your recovery, because I am no role *model or expert in this field. I only know my eating disorder and the struggles that go alongside it. It's the same as trying to answer a maths question: there is only one correct answer, but multiple methods to achieve the same desired end result. Likewise, there is no such thing as a right or wrong way to do recovery; it comes down to what is achievable for you at the time, in correlation with what you want from your life.*

So, all I am able to do is advise you as best as I can, continue supporting you through thick and thin, and keep sending my unconditional love to you regardless of how many miles apart we are.

On a lighter note, I am going to take this opportunity to appreciate every moment I have spent with you, from Pepsi Max trips to our late-night chats. They are cherished memories that have a special place in my heart. 'I will miss you' would be an understatement, but this is not the end of our friendship. It is the beginning of an unbreakable bond that will continue to flourish in the real world. I am proud of you, regardless of what anyone else has to say, and I know you can beat this. I want you to believe this as much as I do. If you are able to overcome this obstacle, nothing else in life will faze you, no matter how big or small. Keep going, lovely!

Dear Kealey,

I didn't think I would be writing this message sitting in a hospital bed right now, but life doesn't fail to surprise us in strange and wonderful ways each day. I am sure you had your eyes set on the goal of becoming a mental health nurse this time last year because helping vulnerable people in their time of need seemed incomparable to any stacks of cash a job could offer.

We were privileged to be under your care, and were gifted with your presence and words of wisdom. The ward will not be the same without you nor could anyone replace you, because there is only one Kealey. I know her as someone who is always up for a laugh, is able to strike the perfect balance between being firm and showing compassion, as well as always sparing an ear for a throttle and still receives you with open arms after every apology. You are an amazing nurse, a trusted friend to many, a loving daughter and, moreover, a kind human being – don't let anyone tell you otherwise!

I am sure you will continue to do great things and inspire many along the way. Although we may no longer be a part of the journey, I cannot wait to hear what the future holds for you, not just in terms of career but in everything life encompasses.

It has been a pleasure getting to know you, seeing you grow in experience and being able to witness the making of a nurse who has saved many lives and will go onto save many more.

Without a doubt, you have set the bar really high (maybe too high). From the bottom of my heart, thank you for being our superhero (batman for Emma) disguised as a caring CSW and, now, nurse. You are an asset to our ward and the NHS as a whole. We need more people like you in this profession so that we can keep our head held high and live up to the motto of consistently trying to "improve lives".

Wish you all the best!
Hopefully we will cross paths again in our future endeavours.

Best wishes,
Gisel xx

To my former, current and future self,

You cannot erase the past, the trauma that you've experienced can't be undone and the pain you've endured can't be minimised.

You've been told countless times to forgive and forget, to not dwell upon it nor let the actions of someone else compromise your future, but it's easy to give such advice as a spectator. When you've been in the frontline, bruised, battered and belittled, it is not so easy to comprehend, let alone forget and move on.

It takes time to rebuild courage, to recuperate the remains of the real Gisel hidden under her armour and to regain the ability to trust people again, even those who you have known for the entirety of your life.

The feeling of loneliness doesn't dissipate when you are surrounded by a crowd of people, it intensifies with the realisation that the crowd is made up of complete strangers who know nothing about you as a person other than the label that has been plastered on you and the past that haunts you. Faces you can't recognise, names you haven't heard before and an unfamiliar environment are the top three ingredients to heighten anyone's anxiety levels and lead to a sense of uneasiness, regardless of whether you suffer from a mental health condition or not.

I was alone yesterday, I am today and I will be tomorrow – that is what my head tells me, again and again.

To a certain extent, when you are miles away from home, a life you've known for so long and the people you love the most, it does very much feel like that.

Here I am, just plopped in the middle of nowhere, treading on unfamiliar grounds and feeling more vulnerable than ever before.

I tilt my head in embarrassment, afraid to look into anyone's eyes and keen in ending conversations before they begin because I am living in fear that the world is against me, the people surrounding me hate me and the ones who supposedly care about me are lying to me.

I look in a mirror hoping to see myself, a true reflection of myself, but instead I see a girl who is hurting, trapped and mortified by the experiences that have sculpted her and every ounce of fat on her. Those are the only things she sees, those are the only things she hears and nothing seems to alleviate this sense of worthlessness.

I would like to say I have come to accept the body I was given, for all its imperfections. The body that didn't give up on me, even at my worst. The body that has enabled me to come this far and will hopefully let me reach where I want to be. However, I haven't, as yet, and that is the harsh reality of living with an eating disorder. Life must carry on regardless. I know this feeling will pass and I will be able to ride it out at some point, maybe not now but hopefully in the future. I need to hold on to that glimmer of hope to spur me on, even in the bleakest of times where I find myself burdened by the troubles of my mind. Otherwise, I will be wandering aimlessly with no future insight.

I know, deep down, this isn't me. This isn't the life I wish to lead. These aren't the dreams I had as a little girl. This isn't the future my family envisioned for me.

Now, I am sat here questioning why I have admitted defeat before the real fight has begun, and why I've not given myself a chance to try and then fail.

There is a fighting spirit within me that I need to unleash. However much I refuse to acknowledge this, I need to face facts. I wouldn't be standing here on this earth, after several unsuccessful suicide attempts, if it was my time to go.

I wake up each morning with my eyelids drooping, my body mentally and physically exhausted from the day before, blindly believing that there is no future for me and that it is better to give up now. But what do I end up doing instead? I wake up each morning able to pick myself up from where I left off and try again, despite what may have happened yesterday. This is because I know for a fact that I can't change the past, as much as I would want to, but every word I mutter and every action I carry out from this point onwards can influence my future.

I still believe that one day I will be able to withstand that demeaning voice in the back of my head and hopefully there will come a day where I am strong enough to silence it, so that I can lead a contented life.

CHAPTER 5

Final thoughts on my struggle

This is dedicated to a person who restored my faith in men and showed me first-hand that there are good people in the world. You just have to go through a few thorns before you find a rose. This man always advised me to surround myself with people worthy of my time and energy; people who appreciate me for everything I've done for them and challenge me, so that I can grow to become the person I aspire to be.

An analogy I came across during my stay as an inpatient is still at the front of my memory and I refer to it every time I meet someone new. There are three major components of a tree: the roots, the branches and then the leaves. Leaves grow to their fullest nearing summer, then lose all of their colour during autumn and fall from the tree during winter, leaving just a bare tree with branches sticking out.

This is similar to those who come and go in your life. They may have been a constant, prominent figure to you during a certain point, but you might have drifted apart or taken two different paths, meaning you were never meant to cross again.

Next are the branches; some can break off easily – you can even snap them off yourself – but others are strong enough to withstand high winds and storms for a bit longer, until they break off, too. The factor that connects both the branches and the leaves is the fact that they don't last forever; the only difference is the time duration and at which point they stopped serving their purpose. Branches are like people in your life that try to be there for you as best as they can, but they have their priorities and their own lives to lead.

They aren't martyrs dedicating every second to be at your side – they are human and that's perfectly okay. As such, they will not always meet your high expectations and you may be left disappointed at times, but this is in no way an adequate indication of their sincerity. Sometimes we just need to acknowledge the fact that life brings up unexpected surprises and unplanned events, which should be dealt with there and then. Despite this, they have helped you through some rough patches. Both of you have encountered a bit of turbulence within the relationship, yet are always up for celebrating all the good times and not afraid to commend each other for doing well. They are more likely to hang around longer than a leaf would and you may still be going strong several years down the line, even if there is only occasional contact. This can easily happen in secondary school, but don't mistake it for five years of friendship going down the drain. As life continues, distance becomes an issue and situations change without you even realising. You will find these connections losing their strength because you are no longer each other's shadows and spend an unhealthy amount of time together. That is not to say that they are not a good friend, family member or acquaintance. They have made an impact that cannot be erased easily – something will trigger a memory associated with them, which will make you remember them from time to time.

Last but not least, you have the roots – the ones that have stuck by you since day one. These are the kind of people who will willingly take any spare second they have to be by your side, either physically, down the phone, in the form of a letter or purely in spirit when you need them most. They can be people who are blood-related, or those who have chosen to be a part of your life. Be grateful for the similarities that unite you and your ever-growing love for each other, whether that be friendship, romantic or otherwise.

Some rules are meant to be broken

We, as a society, are governed by rules and regulations that help bring stability and consensus to an environment, incorporating such a diverse community with various needs and demands. We have to think about both the young and the old, the homeless and those bathing in money, and the rest of us who lay somewhere in between. The only way to do this is by imposing rules that apply to all and can also act as a deterrent if not abided by, no matter where in the hierarchy of classes in society you fall under.

Rules can be a hindrance and act as a way for the anorexia to continue clinging on, although it may seem harmless at the time. I was gullible enough to believe that I was the one in control, when the world around me was constantly changing and I had to sit and watch like a spectator. This was the only aspect in my life that I had control over, or so I foolishly believed. In hindsight, the only purpose it served was to numb my feelings, so that I didn't have to endure the unbearable pain all of the time and avoid life's obstacles in the hope that I would become a nobody. I wanted to be a nobody. I was forced into thinking as though I needed to be one, because life had become unmanageable and this was my deadly secret that would ensure my safety and ultimately keep me sane.

Consequently, this did mean that I forgot what happiness looked like. The great delight and sense of accomplishment I felt after seeing the number drop yet again on the scales was my greatest "happiness" at the time. Nothing was comparable to it: no family occasions, no birthday parties and definitely no memories where my ED wasn't the centre of attention.

Rule 1)
Always try to pick the lowest calorie options from supermarkets, because it is better for your body and your health. The rest are unnecessary calories.

Rule 2)
You have to walk at least 25,000 steps per day. If that means you have to get off the bus nine stops before reaching your destination, then you should do so, otherwise you are being a lazy cow.

Rule 3)
Make sure that you go to the toilet before every weigh day, which does, in turn, mean you will have to incrementally increase your senna (laxative) intake every day. Don't worry, it won't do you any harm and it's done in your best interest, so you can achieve that feeling of emptiness.

Look at what anorexia gives you

You no longer need to suck in your stomach to see your protruding rib cage – anyone can see it, even through the abundant layers of clothes you wear.

You are able to clasp both hands together to fit around your thighs and one hand is enough to grip around your whole upper arm. This means that shopping is limited to the children's section, although, on paper, you are technically a fully-fledged adult. You will always be the odd one out of your friends, who puberty decided to miss out.

The flurry of compliments at the start from everyone surely indicates that you had to lose weight in the first place. You look better now, but only a couple more pounds until you are at your best, right? Wrong. Anorexia carries on until it is satisfied, which unfortunately is never, so whatever you lose is not good enough and never will be.

Yes, you are half the minimum body weight for your height. Yes, your heart is slowly giving up on you, dropping to just 30bpm. Yes, you are hypoglycaemic with a great chance of falling into a coma at any moment. Yes, your hair is falling out in clumps and your scalp is pretty much visible – it is time to say goodbye to your black, long luscious hair. Yes, your bones are as brittle as someone's twice your age, which means you could break them quite easily and it makes you more susceptible to osteoporosis. Yes, Gisel, you are killing yourself, pushing people away and distancing yourself from the real you. Has it ever crossed your mind that your death would tear your family into a million pieces, unable to piece them back together ever again? The genuine smile on your mum's face would cease to exist, your dad would no longer able to hold onto the tears and spend his days and nights in great mourning, your brother would be unable to fill that irreplaceable void in his life and might well fall into the hands of depression as he would be unable to come to terms with losing his only little sister, who was – and still is – his everything.

This is what anorexia will give you and your loved ones. If you carry on, this will become a reality, however extreme it may sound. On the other hand, if you give recovery a go, at least you've got a shot at life.

Despite all of this knowledge, we anorexics still "choose" to carry on with this mentality and "purposely" diminish any speck of hope for a future without our best friend. First and foremost, it needs to be clarified that it is not a choice. Anorexia Nervosa is a deadly illness that creeps into lives during moments of vulnerability. It sucks the life out of you, depriving you of any form of pleasure and leaves you as a shell of a person who doesn't know anything about themselves other than their birth name. It is not self-inflicted, rather it tends to arise due to the involvement of multiple factors from your genetic make-up to the environment you grew up in. Those who take a bit longer to recover are not any less capable or less motivated than those who tend to make what is known as a full recovery in a shorter space of time because of numerous factors – i.e. the right time and the right place. It is hard to predict the struggles that you might encounter on the way; some will be completely out of your hands, so you are better off not comparing yourself to the person next to you who is ready for discharge after a 3-week stay. I have the motivation, the drive, all the incentives in the world, but it's keeping that in mind when I am faced with my worst fear but also my secret pleasure: food. As soon as that plate is put in front of me, to the moment I pick up that knife and fork, my head has experienced the wrath of both world wars all at once. Anorexia is such a deceptive illness that it can change you as a person. This was the case for me. I would go to any extremes to please my anorexia. It became my everything, my heart, my soul and my body from top to bottom.

I could see that I was hurting my family. I could sense their distress and I've even seen my mum bawling her eyes out when she came face to face with me lying on a hospital bed, refusing to take a sip of water. My dad raised his voice; he could no longer bite his tongue and finally perked up the courage to ask, "Why are you so determined to kill yourself?" What hurt the most wasn't the harshness in their words nor the bitterness in their tone, it was the fact that despite all of this commotion around me I still carried on listening to my anorexia. I felt helpless. I wish I could have turned around and told them I deserved to eat, but before those words could even reach the tip of my tongue, I was silenced, yet again, by my anorexia.

One rule that was non-negotiable and took importance above all others was having the element of "control". This control wasn't adequately met in my daily life before I found anorexia. I was craving for this to become a reality for so long that I was prepared to take on anything, even a toxic illness that would lead to torn relationships, wasting away in a psychiatric hospital and could have been the death of me. However, these weren't the promises anorexia had initially made with me, so I am now able to come to the conclusion that anorexia is a pathological liar, able to go to any extremes to get its own way, even if that means taking advantage of vulnerabilities or treading on families that were once stable. It would do so without a speck of remorse. This situation is similar to when you buy something from a shop and as soon as you bring it home, you notice something wrong with it.

Anorexia is a beast. At one point, I became unrecognisable, not just aesthetically, due to the drastic weight loss, but I became a whole new person. Someone who preferred to shut themselves off, was very reserved, unusually shy and not fussed about life, unless it involved the topic of food. These were characteristics that were not generally associated with Gisel, but it perfectly described a person encapsulated by their eating disorder and nothing else – that's who I was. I am not proud to say this nor do I take great joy in announcing that I still struggle immensely with my eating disorder, even on a day-to-day basis, but I have to face facts here, otherwise I am fooling you into thinking recovery is all sunshine and rainbows, which is far from the truth. Just like anything in life, there will be natural fluctuations; at times, the ups may not be as significant as the downs, so we adapt to this and try to find comfort within our suffering, which is not an abnormal reaction to have.

As much as younger Gisel would have liked to prove the doubters wrong, she was still very much engrossed in her eating disorder. She couldn't get her head around the baffling concept that "being three stone heavier would equate to a better life" – how? This is a question to which the answers are obvious for those unaffected, but doesn't make sense to those that are, especially because they are undergoing a torment that doesn't appear to have a pause button.

In a life without anorexia, you have the energy to move as freely as you please, the strength to combat any obstacles in your way, the concentration levels to optimise your chances of passing A levels and your body will start to trust you again, your organs will function accordingly and you will learn how to conquer the fears that once bound you, so that you can finally learn to live and not just survive.

All you need is an inkling that you have a chance at going to university, to build trusted relationships and to enjoy a full life – a life anorexia cannot offer and would never be able to. Trying to break the rules that confine you may seem torturous, especially in the beginning, and there may well be moments where you will scurry back to the safety blanket of anorexia because you know nothing better – it has been your coping mechanism and things won't magically be cured overnight, as much as we wish they would – but with time any wound can heal. Of course, that's not to say that a scab won't form or an infection won't arise, but that's just part of the healing process. So, during recovery, it is important that you shield yourself from potential toxic relationships that could do more damage than good, listen to those who have always had your best interests at heart and don't get too bogged down with the negative ward atmosphere or take on any more burden than you are capable of carrying.

Why is BPD often misinterpreted as a needy self-inflicted illness?

This short extract is quite personal to my current situation, almost five years after being diagnosed with Anorexia Nervosa and this being closely followed by the diagnosis of BPD. The majority of you won't know the meaning of BPD and I am not surprised because until the label was imprinted on me, I was also oblivious apart from hearing it fleetingly in a few conversations. I remember the day I was sat in front of a panel, who only knew me by the notes on a piece of paper, reciting my past history like it was story and describing every incident I had experienced in such grave detail, things I don't even recall. Somehow, they had sculpted a picture of the patient before I walked through the doors. It felt more like an interrogation rather than a tribunal. I was questioned about whether I could keep myself safe enough to be off a section, but whatever I said from that point would be critically analysed and a simple yes wouldn't be satisfactory.

BPD, more commonly known as EUPD (Emotionally Unstable Personality Disorder), is a mental health condition that entrenches all aspects of your life. There is an assumption that BPD patients are dramatic, deceitful and attention-seeking. This means that many health professionals turn a blind eye to the early symptoms of BPD and many go misdiagnosed as having Bipolar or being depressive, which can have a negative impact on their wellbeing. Due to the heavy burden of the stigma, many neglect their treatment or are very uncooperative to therapy sessions or medication, which inevitably results in significant setbacks. These setbacks include plummeting self-confidence and self-esteem, which can trigger a crisis or stem towards other illnesses. However, with the right psychological input, combined with medication, a support network, an understanding of the diagnosis and the ability to apply the skills learnt, many go on to lead normal lives, so it is most definitely a curable illness and there is no need to lose hope.

How to recognise a toxic relationship

It sounds rather simple. When we talk about the failings of a relationship, we automatically direct our thinking towards abuse, affairs and broken trust, which, quite frankly, is not wrong nor am I disregarding the fact that divorce rates are on the rise.

In terms of an inpatient setting, or any place similar to it, toxic relationships are viewed in a very different light. All relationships aren't based around romance; there are fundamental relationships that help to bridge the gap between parents and their children. The success of this is usually dependent on the parenting skills, whether they are a novice or an absolute expert. This is obviously not the case for all, so don't be disheartened new mums and dads! Also, we have siblings by blood and siblings by choice (friends), both of which are important relationships. Also, the relationships I made with some incredible staff members, who were able to chip away my hard armour and uncover bits of the real Gisel during previous admissions, are further examples of important relationships. You will be surprised by the number of bonds created within your lifetime. No type of relationship overrules any others, even if they were created in an unfamiliar place with a bunch of girls of all ages, from every corner of the UK, combating two deadly diseases.

It is so easy to be caught up in the drama of the ward. Surrounding yourself with people who exhibit the same behaviours as you can be quite triggering, but it would be unusual not to make some bonds or form attachments overtime – healthy friendships that could blossom and potentially take flight in the real world. These are the people who you eat with every day for many months, share communal areas with and pretty much live with, so there is very little avoidance and the least you can do is maintain a civilised community.

Friendships formed in these unfortunate circumstances can act as a vessel that will help steer you towards the right direction, by being that person who actually understands because they've had first-hand experience. In this context, though, there is also the need to draw a line and ensure that each of you are not overly involved in one another's care. This is for protection, as both parties are in vulnerable positions. You may sometimes come to the conclusion that there are people who come and go in life, which is perfectly fine, too. It doesn't detract from any of the precious time or effort you both put into building your friendship.

Toxic relationships can be spotted in any area of life, whether it be in a mental health institution or not. The very moment you begin to question the friendship on the basis of mutual respect and whether it is serving a purpose, is when you need to re-evaluate things. In any situation, it is very common to encounter people who you may not instantly gel with or whose personalities clash with yours, but that doesn't mean you can't be good friends.

Before you pour your heart out to someone (including staff), be wary of your surroundings and exempt yourself from any discouraging or negative talk. This is not because I am making assumptions that staff are bad people in any way, I am just prompting you to remember the real reason why you came into hospital. It was not to make friends, but to give you the best chance at recovery. You need to initiate a sense of trust, because the staff members were complete strangers only a couple of days ago and, as harsh as it may sound, you came in on your own and you will walk out of those doors on your own. In some ways, you have to be selfish and you should always evaluate whether a friendship is beneficial from both ends. There should be mutual respect between both individuals.

Ways to spot a toxic relationship

1. Those who only talk to you about calories or food options obsessively, especially when you are not in a place to give anyone advice. I am afraid to say that is not a true friend. It is actually an opportunistic friend, who takes advantage of your knowledge, even though that may have a detrimental impact on their and your mental wellbeing. They are feeding the eating disorder, so that in the long run it's even harder to let go.
2. Peer pressure is an issue among teenagers today, but it is also apparent in mental health units across the country. Within a hospital setting, not everything you hear or see is the truth, so never blindly believe anything. There will be instances where you adopt maladaptive unhelpful behaviours or coping strategies from what others have told you or by witnessing it

take place. Struggles are expected, but if, in any way, you feel directly pressured into doing something that could potentially have a negative impact on you or others, and you wouldn't normally do so otherwise, then that's not a helpful friendship to be a part of any longer.

3. A "two-faced friendship", if that is a real thing. There will be friends that show support when you meet a goal or show signs of progression (i.e. meal completion), but, worryingly, there will also be people that are more eager to talk behind your back about your faults or moments of struggle. They wait patiently for you to slip up and then say, "I knew this would happen". In environments like these, it is hard not to get involved in other people's care and have an opinion about it. People come to a rushed conclusion, perhaps that those who are more vocal about their struggles are putting on a front as a way of seeking attention. However, every action we do has a reaction or consequence to it and that, in itself, is requiring attention. In that sense, we are all attention-seekers. Imagine anorexia as a very competitive group of contestants partaking in a competition and anything less than a win, even if it were to be a tie, is seen as unacceptable. Anorexia engrains a particular way of thinking into the sufferer, so that they carry on losing weight, until one day they disappear. I would strongly advise you to surround yourself with people who bring a positive energy and will support you as best as they can in times of hardship, even if that means taking a step back or seeking help from staff.

I may have missed out quite a few types of toxic friendships, but those are the ones that I am aware of and you will most likely come across, at least once, in an inpatient setting. We are all strangers to one another, cooped up in a psychiatric unit due to mitigating circumstances; we see each other at some of our lowest points and get on each other's nerves at times, but we are made to live with each other regardless.

It is a scary thought, but the voice of anorexia may not completely disappear nor can its thinking pattern be erased permanently from your memory. It's about learning to listen to it and sitting with those feelings, or listening through one ear and letting it go through the other. Living with this illness can be tiring. It can be draining not only for you but for those caring for you. It will require every last remaining bit of strength, even strength you didn't know you had. The less you abide by anorexia's demands, the less control it will have over you.

My life before anorexia

So far we've been focusing on what, how and why anorexia remains in my life and counting the number of wasted years due to it, but what we are failing to see is the life that existed before. Anorexia arrived unexpectedly, like an unwelcome guest, and refused to leave.

I place fond memories from before anorexia close to my heart. For instance, I remember peering through the windows in our flat, eagerly awaiting the ice cream van to pull up. As soon as I had an inkling and could hear it approaching, me and my brother bolted downstairs in record speed. Then, with the remainder of our pocket money, we bought ourselves a 99p Mr Whippy, with a flake and strawberry sauce. It's a combo I would highly recommend to anyone.

Another fond memory of mine also includes food, funnily enough, but the only difference is that it didn't take centre stage. When we (my brother and I) were quite young, we were naive and quite spoilt in some ways, because all our wishes were granted.

The wish that brought the greatest joy to me at the time was my mum coming back from work to kiss me goodnight, with six chicken wings, chips and a fizzy drink. Nothing compared to the satisfaction of sitting in bed, tucking away at our takeaway and watching *Jurassic Park* on repeat on our antenna Panasonic TV. Those were the weekends I looked forward to; those were the days where anorexia was nowhere to be seen. Although I crave for this to be the case again and wish that I could rip out this chapter of my life so that it no longer exists, it is not as simple as that. I can't fix the damage that has been done within, deep within, not visible to the naked eye. Instead, what you can do is set an attainable goal or mini goals to begin with and slowly untangle yourself from this twisted demon.

My family and friends are my life support and I cannot thank them enough for being there, not always in person but definitely in spirit. I know I am in their thoughts all of the time. They watched me bleed; they heard me wail in desperation as I was being thrown around the country as though someone was playing fetch with me. However, they also saw me get up again and again and stand on my own two feet, which just about had the strength to carry the weight of my skeletal body. With it came a broken soul, a deluded mind and a thousand and one burdens to carry around as each day passed.

My early childhood wasn't like this at all. I remember playing in the scorching sun when summer decided to arrive, bickering with my brother about which TV channel to put on next and our countless trips to Morleys (those of you who know will know). I wish I could rewind time – not to do things differently or change what's happened, but to reassure and tell my younger self that she is stronger than she ever thinks, even more than those around her believe and the world mistakenly tells her. This illness makes you feel powerless, but only you can retrieve that power back again. Like one of my lovely friends said to me once, "Don't despair, you are too good for that – believe me, I know!"

CHAPTER 6

What next?

After such a heart-wrenching ordeal as an admission to a psychiatric hospital, each patient has very different ways of coping during the joyous yet unpredictable transition period from hospital to home. The word "discharge" can bring relief for some, knowing that their hard work has finally paid off and they are going on to better things. For others, it can flare up all sorts of emotions, from a sense of accomplishment to being scared and apprehensive about whether they are ready "enough" to try it out on their own in the real world. I can relate to this predicament very much, having experienced it first-hand on repeated occasions.

If you've been an inpatient for an extensive period of time like me, you are bound to make attachments and start trusting those around you to look after you properly. Otherwise, there is no point in being in hospital, because it wouldn't serve the purpose it was set out to achieve or meet your basic needs in terms of care. Just as you are beginning to build a rapport with the staff, enabling you to let your guard down bit by bit and the overwhelming fear of seeking support is slowly but surely starting to subside, you are hit with this predictably unpredictable bombshell. The change was far from wonderful in my eyes and the news that I was moving on in two days was an utter shock to my whole system. My body stiffened in holding onto all the intense feelings I was carrying. I could feel my muscles cramping due to the built-up pressure and uneasiness, tears trickled down my face uncontrollably, so in great desperation I scanned around the room for at least one reassuring nod from a familiar face, but all of the team were as starstruck as I was and lost for words for once. It felt like a hard pill to swallow and I didn't feel as though I was ready to say goodbye, especially not when Bethlem had become my home and the community I warmed to and thought of as my second family. I knew the prospect of further treatment was always on the cards – in fact, I played the role of being my own advocate in fighting for this transition to take place as soon as could be, because I found it incredibly hard to sit with the feeling of uncertainty. The hypothetical discharge plan was always looming in the background, yet postponed for one reason or another, again and again. Therefore, as much as I was the "driving force" for this transfer to happen as soon as possible, there was still a bit of me that didn't think it would happen and I confided in that conclusion. Then, in a matter of minutes, through a single telephone conversation, my fate was decided. The possibility of a transfer was no longer a fantasy. It was becoming a reality and it was just around the corner.

This transfer plan stirred up a lot of difficult thoughts and feelings that I wasn't used to. As a result of this, without me even realising I had my eyes set on relapse and did everything in my power to increase the likelihood of this happening, due to the strong desire to stay within my comfort zone and obtain an element of control again. My reluctance was due to my (justifiable) fear of the unknown, and my worries about whether these complete strangers were supposedly going to give me the best care and would actually live up to my expectations.

As well as feeling reluctant to move on, the thought of actually getting better seemed too far-fetched – and being fourth time lucky, even more so. I had no more tears to spare and the voice I once had was dissipating. With it, the will to live became less and less prominent as each day passed. So, rather than crying all of the time, I was left chuckling at the thought of it and remained sceptical about what the future holds for someone like me, as though I was some sort of abnormal untreatable patient. My head was already fixated on the idea that it would never work out for me and, knowing my luck, I would be digging myself an even bigger hole than before, one I wouldn't be able to climb out of this time.

It is similar to a domino effect, whereby an overriding fear of the unknown and not wanting to let go (which were both perfectly natural reactions to have at the time) contributed to the actions that followed. As much as I was in denial that I was leaving, I knew deep down that it was time for me to move on. Bethlem had offered all the resources in its bag to get me to a stable(ish) position with my eating disorder, so that I could move onto somewhere that would give me the best shot at a full recovery – obtaining a life worth living outside the confinement of hospital walls, outside the restrictions placed by a section and being able to function without the overreliance on medication at such a young age.

During this particularly rough patch, I had to keep reiterating to myself that this is in no way is a true reflection of who I am, even though it seemingly fits that "overly needy, attention-seeking" character that BPD had falsely painted over the real me. It is fair to say I found great comfort in the thought of staying at Bethem, because that was all I knew and I was too susceptible to any form of change, let alone moving over 130 miles away from where I called home and the people I called family. To no one's surprise, I was trembling with fear, especially in my last few days there. Who wouldn't be after an almost 15-month stay and then being told, last-minute, that you are leaving?

Every time I wrote a goodbye card, I couldn't help but shed a tear. From being in the frontline cheering the transfer on, then switching all of a sudden to the opposite side of the spectrum. I hated the feeling of moving – despised it, in fact. All I could do to help myself at that point was to take on board everything people around me (who I knew cared) had advised, whether I wholeheartedly believed it or not at the time. This was the first step towards me acknowledging that I am only human and these feelings are justified, in no way abnormal or entirely my fault. There will be times in everyone's lives where these bottled-up emotions come crashing down all at once, like a wobbly Jenga tower, and the first thing you witness is the aftermath and the mess it leaves. However, always remember that this is not the end; you can still pick the pieces up and rebuild the tower again – the tower of resilience, I call it in this case. The only difference is that this time around, it will be better and sturdier than before, able to withstand those little sways from side to side and remain standing tall. This is because you know the aim, what is expected of you and you have more skills in your pocket that will aid your overall victory. There may be falls, plenty of them, but it is how you approach them afterwards and not let it become an obstacle for you to try again.

That is how I ended up reassuring myself each day, having recently spent my fourth consecutive birthday in hospital. Otherwise, I am left with no hope, less likely to be receptive to any treatment and, forty years down the line, I may still be spending my birthdays within the confinement of a hospital ward. Four years may seem like a lifetime for a 19-year-old, but in the grand scheme of things it is only a brief chapter of the book, which encompasses your entire life. A book whereby you are the author, editor and publisher. You have the power to change the ending or create an unexpected plot twist for the better.

It is hard to all of a sudden be plucked out from a community that you finally felt a part of and become like a second family to them. Over a period of time, you were even able to build trusted relationships between staff and patients, which you thought would never exist. You had plenty of laughs, as well as a fair few cries. It may not have been the most memorable time of your life, being cooped up in a psychiatric hospital, but it was still a memory – one that, during times of hardship, you will fondly look back on, remembering every helpful piece of advice. You may have heard multiple times to not look back, because you are not going that way and in no way am

I disagreeing with this rationale (entirely), but sometimes you have to look back to recognise how far you have come in your journey and give yourself that little bit of credit you deserve. Every experience teaches you a lesson: some are more obvious than others, some will pop into your head every so often and others will be treasured for the rest of your life. In my opinion, there is something you can always reflect upon or wish you did differently, but what would be the consequence of that, because there are so many 'what ifs?' in life. Being an inpatient is hard in itself, but you can be so easily caught up with any bad experiences associated with hospitals and so overly focused on what you've lost (temporarily!). For example, being restricted of life's simple necessities, which many in the outside world take for granted, and every step and action being monitored and scrutinised regardless of whether you are a fully-fledged adult. At times, it felt as though both my hands were tied to my back, my eyes blindfolded and my mouth plastered shut, unable to hold onto any fraction of hope or see the outside world as the key to opening doors of opportunities. It is easy for a spectator to say, "Don't look at the transition as something daunting, but rather a step in the right direction." But after being in hospital for so long, it becomes your comfort zone without you realising and so moving on seems impossible to imagine. It is no different from the mixed emotions and stresses that come alongside moving out from a family home you grew up in.

I am saying the following with full confidence, having experienced being thrown around like a toy from unit to unit all across the country in desperation to find the perfect one: there is no magical cure for this illness, nor is there the "perfect" unit that will cater for all of your needs, because needs can change, as can presentations. This illness can manifest in ways you've never seen or experienced.

It was so easy for me to pass the blame onto the hospital and the clinicians for being the "hindrance" to carrying on my life in the outside world. I remember questioning them and demanding an answer as to why they were punishing me for something I couldn't control. However, any answer they provided me with would have sounded illogical to anorexia and this beastly illness would never have been satisfied. What I failed to recognise at the time was that everything they did was with my best interests at heart and they would never commit to this type of profession if they found pleasure in seeing others suffer – quite the opposite actually.

Your prospect of a better future is closer than you think, and the hospital and the responsible caregivers weren't the reason why you lost everything you worked so hard for. The culprit is the deceptive illness that doesn't seem to leave your side. So, don't direct your anger and anguish towards those caring for you. Instead, direct your anger and anguish towards your illness, so that you can break free of the shackles that once bound you and the restrictions that anorexia placed upon you.

When I entered Bethlem for the first time, I was bemused, lost and forgotten (similar to how I feel now in this new environment). I thought that those feelings would never subside and I would never be able to establish any sort of therapeutic relationship with the staff. I couldn't see myself talking to anyone, let alone becoming friends with other patients.

Each one of the patients and members of staff were complete strangers until 6th of July 2018 (my readmission date), but I have come to realise how privileged I was to have known them, regardless of the circumstances. They became my biggest life support during times of trouble and we were a unit, a family unit with an unbreakable bond who carried each other along when we didn't have the strength to do it ourselves. It didn't seem like I had only known them for 15 months, but more so the entirety of my life. The friendships I built got me through some of the bleakest times, when I thought there wasn't a way back. They made me realise that there are people out there who feel the things I feel, that have experienced the things I've experienced and still manage to hold onto that little bit of light at the end of the tunnel. They were the best cheerleaders and advice-givers, who continued supporting and encouraging me no matter what time of day it was, who never doubted my ability even once and urged me to keep plodding on even when I thought I couldn't take another step forward.

I won't be able to unsee some of the things I witnessed in the first place, though, like patients being restrained and dragged against their will to the clinic room and pinned down to have an Ng feed (the most dreaded time of the day for any anorexic). There are also things I would never have liked to hear, such as patients helplessly crying and screaming at the top of their lungs when they found themselves amongst a crowd of strangers eager to pull their trousers down and forcefully injecting them as though they were a feral animal.

My experiences in inpatient settings haven't been the easiest, but I have met some incredible, strong-willed individuals, who I knew from day one had everything it takes to regain control of their lives. There were also some whose battle seemed to be never-ending even after an admission, but the hard work they put in to get past that barrier that had been blocking them for so long was inspiring to watch.

This isn't the end, but only the beginning of a new chapter in my life – one that will hopefully allow me to flourish and continue on the path to recovery, despite the setbacks in between. Once again, I am going to reiterate that Anorexia Nervosa is a deadly mental illness that needs just as much attention and acknowledgement as any other physical ailment.

The only advice I can give you is that a "happily ever after" is almost impossible to obtain, not because you are incapable of it in any way, though. It's simply due to the fact that we are all human and are prone to making mistakes here and there. I also don't want you to mistakenly think that everything will remain doom and gloom forever either, because with time things do change. The power is in your hands to alter the future so that you never have to revisit the past. We shouldn't pin all our hopes, successes and this "happily ever after" ending on the basis of the career we pursue, being in a happy relationship, having children, money to spare and a house to call your own, but rather on whether these bonds and materialistic items provide you with the joy you had always hoped for and that anorexia could never replace. Life after anorexia shouldn't solely be based on how you do in the above aspects. I am not denying the fact that these can play a part, even a major part, and act as the stimulus or initiator for recovery to become a reality. However, from my point of view, real recovery from anorexia is more to do with learning to love yourself for who you are with all your attributes, little quirks and imperfections – everything else is secondary to this.

Learn to accept the body you were given; every scar on your arm shows your story and every tear shed shows how courageous you are. I sometimes wish I could reverse time and undo the damage that has already been done. Sometimes I wish I could erase the past and start all over again from the minute I was born up until now. Sometimes I wish I didn't have to dwell in self-pity and punish myself for something I wasn't even the culprit of. Sometimes I wish I didn't have to live every minute of my life in ambivalence about the future. I simply wish I was me, Gisel Josy, not an emotionally fragile girl unable to piece together a life of her own, unpossessed by her illnesses. Unfortunately, that is who I am today... but not who I wish to be tomorrow.

Talking about grief

Here I stand in great stillness and solemnity in front of your grave, forcing myself to say a premature goodbye. My heart is crippled at the thought of not waking up another morning with a "Good morning hun xx" message. I cannot deny the fact that I am still stuck in utter disbelief. There are questions spiralling within my head, around and around again. How could this happen? More importantly, how could I let this happen and why not me instead? Then, all of a sudden, I feel an itch under my skin that persists for some time, before it is taken over by a rush of anger towards this wretched illness.

I could easily use some foul language to describe this illness to a T, and that's saying it politely, but I am not going to lower myself to its standards. If this was the hunger games, I would sacrifice myself instead of you without an inkling of doubt, but I am afraid that this is life and I am channelling this anger, as the fire in my belly, to keep me going even when I feel like crumbling. You will be remembered as Hayley Smith. We rejoice in all your triumphs, take pride in the commendable fight you displayed each day without fail and remember you for the extraordinarily brilliant qualities you had that sculpted the person you were. The loving daughter, aunty, older sister and friend you were to so many – these titles will never be stripped from you and are incomparable to any "accomplishment" that this illness had gifted you with.

As much as I tried to rally in the emotions to prevent myself from becoming a blubbering mess again, especially in front of sixty other unfamiliar faces, I couldn't help but feel a surge of sadness overtake me when the coffin was in sight. Before I knew it, tears started trickling down my face, one by one. Then, all of a sudden, tears were gushing out like a waterfall; all the effort I had put into pretending I was absolutely fine went down the drain and the guard I had put up was ripped into shreds in a matter of minutes. What I forgot to acknowledge was that it was completely natural and more than healthy to cry in that instance. It was a part of grieving and losing someone that meant an awful lot to you. As much as I would have loved to recompose myself and be there for the other girls and not just wallow in my own sorrows, I just didn't have it in me to do so and that, at the time, seemed very selfish of me. I knew, deep down, that no one expected anything of me, not any of my friends, Hayley's family nor

Hayley for that matter, but I enforced that expectation upon myself. In DBT, we refer to this as judgemental thinking, which is mainly to do with criticising ourselves for things that may not be within our control. In hindsight, I could have effectively combated this "thought", the emphasis being put on it as a thought and NOT a fact with radical acceptance. I had to accept the reality that Hayley had passed away and there was nothing I could do about it, whether I wanted to or not.

a) Rejecting reality does not change it nor does it make it any easier for me to tolerate the pain associated with the loss.
b) Therefore, pain quickly evolves into suffering and self-critical thinking, as though somehow this was all avoidable and the power was in my hands when, in actual fact, I am not even in the picture.
c) So, the question now arising is, "Why am I blaming myself?" The path out of hell is through misery and I have every right to grieve healthily, which entails not putting my wellbeing at risk, too, because the Hayley I knew wouldn't wish this upon anyone, even her worst enemy.
d) Pain is inevitable in life and doesn't always correlate to a life not worth living, but suffering is optional and caused by a refusal to accept the pain for what it is.
e) Refusal to accept grief = long-standing bitterness, anger and resentment.
f) I decided to harness this anger and direct it towards the anorexia and PD. I almost felt like I possessed a superpower, which spurred me on to make Hayley proud in everything I did from that moment forward, whether it was as little as eating an extra chip to just letting myself sit with uncomfortable emotions rather than acting on them impulsively and regretting my erratic decision later on.

This is a poem I wrote to myself and I would like to share regardless of whether you can relate to it or not. At some point in our lives it's inevitable that we will cross paths with death, whether it be for someone dear to us or someone you happened to know. The unexpected deaths can be the hardest to comprehend and adjust to; no death is easy, but it's the only guaranteed event on Earth. All I know is that Hayley is not going to spend even a second longer being tormented by her demons and she can finally rest in eternal peace. Never forgotten. She holds a special place in my heart and in the memories we shared together, which I will forever cherish.

The void is irreplaceable, the damage is done
I cannot comprehend the reason behind
why you had to be the one
I wish I could go back and hug you one last time
But this deceptive illness told us that you were just fine.

It took us all by surprise when you lay there so still,
in such peace I've never witnessed until.
I imagine that you are finally spreading
your wings my angel,
flying high up above the sky,
away from this troublesome uncanny world
that gave you nothing but grief
stocked up with an unlimited supply of
coffee for all your mischief.

The time is fast approaching for us to say goodbye
If I could sacrifice myself I would without a second
thought, but I live in consolation that "Oh my darling
you damn well fought."

This is a poem I would like to share composed by my dear
friend Kieron:

Hope

It's as though my thoughts,
are obscured by smoke.
They turn to words and sting my throat,
the thing about hard times is that,
It's harder to look forward than back.

But I must, and in myself I trust,
so when my heart's in pieces, and
my mind turns to dust,
I turn to hope, to cope.

Each day you wake, each step you take,
is proof of what your soul can take,
so keep in mind, the strength you'll find.
There's peace of mind, in looking in the mirror,
and choosing to be kind.

Existing vs Living

LIMERICK

She frantically searched around the room,
To find a way to escape from the doom,
Whilst the dreaded scale,
Called her a big whale,
When all she wanted was to bud and bloom.

SONNET

Sadness thrived in the absence of hope while,
Cooped up within the constraints of four walls,
Where I was made to feel deranged and small,
All I wanted was to regain my smile.

It felt like I ran a thousand miles,
Now weary, worn out, unable to crawl,
Used to be able to stand up so tall,
Now it feels like I live in exile.

I looked at myself in utter disgust,
Face to face with the monster I became,
Stony gaze, gaunt face, drained of all colour.

Realising all my dreams had turned to dust,
And surely I was the one to blame,
How did my life become this much crueller?

The love I used to have....

When I used to look in the mirror, I was content with the reflection I saw. No, it wasn't perfect... far from it, in all honesty. The stretch marks seeped through my ripped jeans, the rolls rippled down my stomach and I didn't think twice about flaunting my double chin when I was asked to do a silly pose for a photo. I simply brushed off the disconcerting looks I got from others or I thought I did, but before I knew it all the piercing stares, snarky remarks and uneasy talk came to bite me in the head. I started questioning every inch of my body, from the tips of my toes to the top of my head, home to my scraggly hairs. I cringed at the sight of me when I accidently caught my reflection in a mirror, but I still looked anyway, hoping I would find an angle I didn't despise as much. Surprise, surprise! I had no luck whatsoever, so I simply walked away, bowing my head in utter disgust, asking myself how I let myself become this way again.

I shrivelled into a body of a ten-year-old, dress sizes dropping as fast as a ball thrown from a great height; my hair fell out in clumps, clogging up the shower every time I could brave a shower and stand to look at my naked self. Every step I took became more of a struggle because my feeble body was ready to collapse at any moment and I was unsure of whether the next inhale of breath was to be my last. However, my only wish at the time was to waste away. I tried to disguise the ever-growing hatred I had for my body by piling on the clothes, tampering with my weight so that my secret was kept, skipping the occasional meal to going days on an empty stomach, my breath reeking, my eyelids drooping and my eyes growing heavy, overtaken by sheer exhaustion. Losing weight soon became an addiction I couldn't get a handle of; seeing the number drop on the scales gave me a thrill I hadn't experienced before and soon my wardrobe shrank in half before my eyes, similar to the remainder of what you could call my body. Not only did I lose the love I had for my body, I lost being able to undergo normal bodily functions, allowing me to walk upright with my head held high, see the world around me with open eyes, smell freshly cut grass and even the somewhat refreshing polluted London air, touch and embrace the warmth of family cuddles and be able to enjoy the taste of delicious home comforts again.

My safe place

Everyone has a safe place in their mind that they can confide in during times of distress or emotional dysregulation. If you haven't found yours yet, I highly recommend you think of one right now. Imagery and visualisation can transport you to a whole new world. It cannot erase how you are feeling, but it can take your mind off things for a short period of time until things begin to de-escalate and you are more in control. I will share mine with you: my grandma's house all the way in India.

I am rocking back and forth in my chair, basking in the glorious sunshine. I can feel the humidity itching under my skin, causing an uncomfortable sticky sensation. I almost feel like a melting popsicle in this heat. Then, all of sudden, the sun subsides for a bit and I can hear the pitter patter of the raindrops against the windowpane. The large pillows of clouds reform, blotting out droplets as big as the size of a satsuma, and it almost sounds as though the heavens have finally erupted. The drops start to fade into a musical chime, as I sit among my family in the comfort of my family home, somewhere where I felt I belonged.

What is a life worth living?

For those of you who have done/attempted dialectical behaviour therapy (DBT), or engaged in some form of therapy closely linked to DBT such as RO DBT, and also for those working within the field, the term "a life worth living" can be a go-to term that many therapists get into the habit of regurgitating. Therefore, it is no surprise that many of you may have misunderstood it or been told numerous definitions by qualified professionals that are trained in DBT. I am not going to sit here and claim to have the right definition or the magic solution, nor am I a qualified DBT therapist. I am simply Gisel Josy, an emotionally fragile 20-year-old, combating the demons that have tormented me for an unjustifiably long time, while piecing together a life for myself outside the four walls of a psychiatric hospital. This is the perspective I will provide you with today and if that helps even one single person reading this, then that's a job well done in my eyes.

If we lived in a world that accepted mental health for what it is, we wouldn't notice it. Just like if we were to be born in a world with people who were predominately deaf or blind, or even both, we wouldn't know anything else. In an ideal world, mental health would not be classed as a taboo topic. It should be talked about just like we would speak about a broken leg or a cold to a friend or a health professional. No one should be afraid to speak out because of the overlying fear of being shamed or overlooked. During my time in treatment, I have acquired many skills that have led me onto the path to true recovery with the aid of a truly amazing therapist (Ki). She told me to always remain skilful, even in unfavourable circumstances, and always ask what is the most effective thing to do and whether it would be beneficial to the interaction and, ultimately, would it make things worse? Be willing to negotiate, radically accept change and always think of the next best feeling. The only thing you are in control of is YOU and you will always have your breath. So, breathe mindfully, half smile when you feel irritated or distressed, or when you know things are about to spiral out of control, pace breathe (I breathe in for 5 seconds, out for seven seconds, or box breathe by breathing in for four seconds, holding for four seconds and breathing out for four seconds) and power pose. Power posing is when you stand in a posture that you associate with being powerful, perhaps with your hands on your hips, straight back, head held high in the hope that you feel and behave more assertively. Studies have shown that it is proven to reduce cortisol levels – a hormone related to stress – and increase testosterone. If you are interested in finding out more about power posing, I highly recommend watching Amy Curdy's TED talk.

So, next time you have an urge for self-harm, make sure you use the STOP skill:

S – Stop when you feel as though your emotions are getting on top of you. Don't react. Don't move a muscle. Freeze!

T – Take a step back. Give yourself some time to calm down and think rationally. Unstick yourself from what's going on around you and take deep breaths to ensure that you are the one in control.

O – Observe what is happening around you, who is involved and how everyone is interacting towards one another. Do not jump to conclusions. In order to make the wisest and most effective choice, use mindfulness skills of observing and a non-judgemental attitude.

P – Proceed mindfully. Ask yourself, "What do I want from this situation? Would what I am about to do make it better or worse?" Do the opposite action if need be. If you feel like punching the wall, sit on your hands, be mindful and do not act impulsively or act without thinking, because I can assure you, you will regret it in the long run.

These are only a handful of the skills that I learnt in DBT and I hope it is somewhat useful to you. It is not only applicable to someone suffering from a mental health condition but anyone living the daily stresses of life. It will ultimately lead you to (you guessed it) a life worth living!

Transferring between hospitals – hospital to home

Cygnet Coventry Hospital was not just a roof over my head for the past ten months, but a home for me where I felt a sense of belonging. It was scrutinised, disregarded as inadequate and eventually forced to shut down. Yes, it had its ups and downs; yes, it wasn't the perfect place that accommodated all our needs; yes, there were areas that needed improvement, but for all I know every staff member (with maybe a few exceptions) went above and beyond their limits to help us onto the road to recovery.

However impossible it may have seemed, they held hope for us when we couldn't do so ourselves, they reassured us that things would be okay in the end if we set our minds to it (because the power is ultimately within our grasp), they made us laugh our heads off with their ridiculous jokes, they wound up us up when we didn't get what we wanted and they cheered us up even in times of distress.

Dear Cygnet Coventry,
It has been a turbulent journey, to say the least, and I can't quite believe it has come to a close now. I have met some incredible individuals, both within the hospital and outside. I wish I could go back in time and change things and not self-sabotage like I usually do, because I am too afraid that people won't stay or like me for who I am. I wish I could tell myself that I am strong enough to fight this, even when the whole world turned against me and told me I was

worth nothing more than the dirt under my feet. I wish I was able to count my blessings more, rather than dwell on the past and from now on that is what I will strive to do. This is a new chapter in my journey, one in which I will conquer my demons, refuse to give up even when I feel exhausted and I will be the one in control at last. Here's to new beginnings.

The end that welcomes a new beginning

I will end by saying my final goodbye to anorexia, which has shaped me to become the stronger person I am today, able to withstand any obstacle that comes along the way, but the enormity of the grief and pain that it has inflicted upon me is incomparable to the strength that I have gained. For that I would not wish this upon anyone, not even my worst enemy, and I hope that those who are suffering can see that there is some light at the end of the tunnel, despite the fact that it may look bleak right now. Remember to hold on: pain ends; nothing is forever.

Dear Anorexia, my enemy,

I have salvaged the strength to write this letter today on the 6th of May − the day I became informal − because I know you are no longer a part of me. You were my best friend, my shoulder to lean on when I was weak, my legs to carry me when I couldn't bear to do so myself. You were my everything, but from this day forth you will be stripped of that title and valued as little as the dirt under my feet. You promised me love that I never received, acceptance that I never achieved and respect that I never gained. In fact, all you gave me was a bundle of false promises. My eyes were sealed, you blinded me; my ears were forced shut, you deafened me; my legs were tied together, you made me lame; my voice was stolen, you made me mute; but now I am free. It's my time to redeem what I have lost and show you that you are no longer in charge of me. I've burst through the flames stronger than ever before, dusted myself off after every fall, and black and white has turned to colour now. I can hear the sound of my own voice without it being overpowered by yours. I can look in the mirror and stand tall with my head held high and see that freedom is an open door. I am living now.

I believe wholeheartedly that what anorexia has to offer me is incomparable to the great potential I have, the life I have going for me and the world awaiting me outside. So, I opened my eyes, put a gentle smile back on my face and in my darkest times knew that I would survive. I am Gisel Josy, not my illness... nor the illness that once consumed me.

Goodbye, at last, anorexia. I wish to never cross paths with you, not now, not tomorrow, not ever again.

Dear body,

Forgive me for the torture I put you through, forgive me as I never wanted to hurt you and forgive me for refusing to listen when all you yearned for was to be heard.

Now, I thank you for not giving up on me when I gave up on myself.

Thank you for piecing me together after I shred you into a million pieces.

Thank you for giving me the energy to continue fighting each day. You were the true warrior here because without you I would have never won this battle. Now, you are mine and I am yours. Now, we don't have to fight against each other. We are in unison. Now, I have learned to listen to all your needs like you are my own and cradle you in my arms, because I was wrong.

How it feels to finally be free

Today is the day, the day I've been waiting for so long – days, months, even years have passed and I have become more and more hesitant to believe that this day would ever arrive. The last five years spent in hospital, the struggles I have endured and the tears I've shed have not been in vain and today is the day that has brought it to light. I am free at last, ready to spread my wings and take flight for the first time. I know I might stumble along the way; there may well be setbacks, but that doesn't mean I have to start from square one again. It simply means I have to stop, breathe and carry on going regardless. I am DISCHARGED! This is a feeling that will prevail for some time, a feeling I would like to cling onto during times of doubt, a feeling that will aid me in continuing to recover outside the four walls of a psychiatric hospital where alarms blast out loud, cries bellow down the corridors, blood stains are imprinted on the walls like some sort of decoration and people aimlessly walk down the corridors with no sense of where they are or what they are doing. I will never forget those days; they were my past, but they do not have to be my future. I am eternally grateful to everyone who has been at my side along the way, from a simple text message to sitting down next to me in restraint, or trying your utmost to stop me from hurting myself.

Thank you, and here is to my new beginning, one in which I will make each one of you proud and, most importantly, myself.

Acknowledgements

I would also like to take this opportunity to thank my family, my friends and every individual along the way who has helped me onto the road to recovery. Without them, I wouldn't be able to tell the tale about my old friend anorexia and I most certainly wouldn't be capable of leading the life I had always dreamt of. This isn't the end, only the beginning to rejoice and thrive in the real world until next time. I hope that you all stay strong and beat the demons that once consumed you. Remember that you are not alone. We cannot stop the wind, but we can direct the boat and keep the eye on the end goal, so that we don't lose control.

Hope is the first step to resolving any problem; without it, we are only left with chaos. So, persevere; every problem no matter how big or small has a solution, you have just got to find it. I was once bruised, battered and belittled because the whole world told me I was never going to get up. The whole world told me I was insignificant and I would lose this battle, so there was no point in retaliating. After all, the whole world was my anorexia.

But look at me now, surviving – no, thriving – and I'm never going to turn back because life is so much better now.

About the author

Gisel Josy is a 21-year-old woman who has recovered from Anorexia Nervosa and borderline personality disorder (BPD). Although she has spent countless years in hospital, Gisel has managed to finally conquer her demons. By sharing her mental health recovery, she hopes to help others who are struggling. She has accepted her past and is hopeful of what the future may hold. www.healingtakestimedotblog.wordpress.com

About Cherish Editions

Cherish Editions is a bespoke self-publishing service for authors of mental health, wellbeing and inspirational books.

As a division of Trigger Publishing, the UK's leading independent mental health and wellbeing publisher, we are experienced in creating and selling positive, responsible, important and inspirational books, which work to de-stigmatise the issues around mental health and improve the mental health and wellbeing of those who read our titles.

Founded by Adam Shaw, a mental health advocate, author and philanthropist, and leading psychologist Lauren Callaghan, Cherish Editions aims to publish books that provide advice, support and inspiration. We nurture our authors so that their stories can unfurl on the page, helping them to share their uplifting and moving stories.

Cherish Editions is unique in that a percentage of the profits from the sale of our books goes directly to leading mental health charity Shaw Mind, to deliver its vision to provide support for those experiencing mental ill health.

Find out more about Cherish Editions by visiting cherisheditions.com or by joining us on:

Twitter @cherisheditions
Facebook @cherisheditions
Instagram @cherisheditions

Cherish
EDITIONS

About Shaw Mind

A proportion of profits from the sale of all Cherish Editions books go to their sister charity, Shaw Mind, also founded by Adam Shaw and Lauren Callaghan. The charity aims to ensure that everyone has access to mental health resources whenever they need them.

You can find out more about the work Shaw Mind do by visiting their website: shawmind.org or joining them on

Twitter @Shaw_Mind

Facebook @shawmindUK

Instagram @Shaw_Mind

Your Local Mental Health & Wellbeing Charity

Lightning Source UK Ltd.
Milton Keynes UK
UKHW040859310123
416235UK00005B/169

9 781913 615116